Library of
Davidson College

QUINTET

Books by Robert Manson Myers

HANDEL'S MESSIAH: A TOUCHSTONE OF TASTE (1948)
(New Edition, 1971)

FROM BEOWULF TO VIRGINIA WOOLF (1952)
(New Edition, Revised, 1984)

HANDEL, DRYDEN, AND MILTON (1956)

RESTORATION COMEDY (1961)

THE CHILDREN OF PRIDE (1972)
(New Edition, Abridged, 1984)

A GEORGIAN AT PRINCETON (1976)

QUINTET (1991)

QUINTET

A Five-Play Cycle
Drawn from
The Children of Pride

ROBERT MANSON MYERS

With an Introduction by
Patti P. Gillespie

University of Illinois Press
Urbana & Chicago

Copyright © 1991 by Robert Manson Myers
Introduction © 1991 by the Board of Trustees
of the University of Illinois
Manufactured in the United States of America
C 5 4 3 2 1
This book is printed on acid-free paper.

CAUTION

Professionals and amateurs are hereby warned that these plays, being fully protected under the copyright laws of the United States of America, the British Commonwealth, including Canada, and all other countries subscribing to the Berne and Universal Copyright Conventions, are subject to royalty. All rights, including professional, amateur, motion picture, recitation, lecturing, public reading, radio and television broadcasting, and translation into foreign languages, are strictly reserved. Particular emphasis is laid on the question of readings, permission for which must be secured from the publisher in writing. All inquiries concerning rights should be addressed to The University of Illinois Press, 54 East Gregory Drive, Champaign, Illinois 61820.

LIBRARY OF CONGRESS CATALOGING-IN-PUBLICATION DATA

Myers, Robert Manson, 1921–
  Quintet : a five-play cycle drawn from The children of pride / by Robert Manson Myers ; with an introduction by Patti P. Gillespie.
    p. cm.
    Contents: The courtship of Mary Jones—A Georgian at Princeton—Voices of pride—The courtship of Carrie Davis—The night season.
    ISBN 0-252-01751-X (alk. paper)
    1. Jones, Charles Colcock, 1804–1863—Family—Drama. 2. United States—History—Civil War, 1861–1865—Drama. 3. Georgia—History—Civil War, 1861–1865—Drama. 4. Reconstruction—Georgia—Drama. 5. Jones family—Drama. I. Children of pride. II. Title.
PS3563.Y455Q56 1991
812'.54—dc20   90-31828
                                                                         CIP

In Memoriam
David Lloyd Kreeger
(1909–1990)

CONTENTS

Introduction by Patti P. Gillespie
ix

The Courtship of Mary Jones
3

A Georgian at Princeton
59

Voices of Pride
101

The Courtship of Carrie Davis
155

The Night Season
207

Introduction

Patti P. Gillespie

In October 1985 the city of Savannah, Georgia, briefly captured a rare and much-valued theatrical experience—a true community theatre. The occasion was the world premiere of *Quintet*. Performed in the Savannah Theatre, one of America's oldest surviving playhouses, the plays were accompanied by lectures, tours, and civic celebrations remarkable for their excellence. Among the several hundred people gathered for this five-day festival were professional historians, literary critics, theatre scholars, tourists, and locals. They came from places as far away as Maine and California and as near as Liberty County, Georgia. I was invited by *Theatre Journal* to cover the event, and so I recorded my own reactions in some detail:

> The binding force of the experience was unquestionably Myers's book, *The Children of Pride*, winner of *The New York Times Book Review* Award for 1972 and the National Book Award for 1973.... Following the triumph of this book Myers set for himself a second formidable task: from the Joneses' letters alone he set about to shape a series of five plays, each with a coherent action compressible to about two hours. The resulting plays are, with a single exception, one- and two-character pieces in which dramatic action—and interaction—give way to recitations, alternatively motivated as letter writings, letter readings, and free reminiscences. The challenge to the actors and directors is therefore quite formidable, for they are asked to vivify extended lyric and expository passages written a century ago by Southerners who, although exceedingly cultured and articulate, sought familial solidarity, not dramatic art.
>
> In performance, the power of the whole proved greater than the power of any one of its parts. The cycle invited the audience to reflect on the

complexity of the human condition, the intricacy and delicacy of democratic social covenants, and the suffering of all people when the convulsions of war seize the body politic. Indeed, the appeal of the cycle lies in large measure with characters who repeat from play to play, acting out familiar cultural myths, displaying the hard lessons that no generation escapes the errors of its ancestors, that no age contradicts the legacy of its past, that no culture sees itself hurtling toward disaster until the disaster is upon it.

Quintet is clearly no ordinary work. Distant from the slick comedies and splashy musicals that comprise today's commercial American theatre, *Quintet* invites quiet reflection—about our national past, our changing values, our uncertain future. Its scope is grand, its pace leisurely, its language eloquent. How such a proudly— even stubbornly—different work came to be produced intrigued me, and so after returning from Savannah I sought out its history:

Robert Manson Myers, native Virginian and professor of English, published *The Children of Pride* in 1972. This exceptional book, fashioned from more than six thousand pieces of correspondence exchanged among members of the Jones family of Liberty County, Georgia, in the years surrounding the Civil War, is an epic work of almost two thousand pages. Critics hailed it as "an epistolary novel," as "extraordinary social history," as "an American *War and Peace.*" *The New York Times Book Review* perhaps described it best: "No story in America's history has been so often told, or has so well stood the retelling, as that of the Old South and its destruction. But Robert Manson Myers's splendid *The Children of Pride* tells it as it has not been told before, in the fullness of its poignance and tragedy."

Even before the publication of this book Myers had detected in the Joneses' letters the seeds of drama; and so, soon after completing the novel, he began to weigh the possibilities of retelling the Joneses' story for the stage. An invitation to read sections of his book for Chicago's Fortnightly Club in November 1972 transformed the possibility into reality.

The first play to be completed (although the final play of the published cycle) was *The Night Season,* a monodrama from the letters of Mary Jones, family matriarch, mother of three children, and mistress of three plantations. For the first performance of the play at the Fortnightly Club, Myers himself interpreted the role of Mary Jones. The audience's response was encouraging; a spectator wrote: "It was a remarkable evening.... We found it spellbinding. One sensed for the first time a manner in which complex forces... resolved to mold the character of these prideful people, made them both admirable and despicable, strong and weak." (Other readings followed—at Cambridge University, at several American universities, at the Folger Shakespeare Theatre, and, in 1980, on BBC Radio 3.) This play's clear success added to Myers's growing conviction that creditable translations from the letters to the stage were indeed possible. He therefore began to shape a second play in 1974.

The Courtship of Mary Jones, drawn from letters exchanged by Mary Jones and her cousin Charles Colcock Jones in 1829–1830, portrays these two young people as they prepared for matrimony. During their eighteen-month separation (while he attended Princeton Theological Seminary), they wrote each other of Christian faith and loving devotion, thus offering the background against which the ultimate collapse of their world can be assessed. As first produced by Ted Walch at Washington's Trapier Theatre in July 1976, *The Courtship of Mary Jones* attracted favorable notice from *The Washington Post,* which praised the play's "vivid characters."

Encouraged, Myers began work on his third play, *Voices of Pride,* crafted from the correspondence of Charles and Mary Jones and their two adult children, Charles C. Jones, Jr., and Mary Sharpe Jones. Produced in June 1977, again by Walch and the Trapier Theatre, this play likewise earned the praise of *The Washington Post:* "Ted Walch, Trapier's director, brings the letter colloquy to the stage with dramatic impact." A fourth play quickly followed. *A Georgian at Princeton,* another monodrama, drew on the letters of Charles C. Jones, Jr., also the source of Myers's second epistolary novel, published in 1976 under the same title.

The first opportunity to produce the plays as a cycle, in this case a tetralogy, came in 1982. In celebration of the tenth anniversary of the publication of *The Children of Pride,* Ken Yellis (Curator of Education at the National Portrait Gallery, Smithsonian Institution) offered the four existing plays in rapid repertory. Opening with *The Courtship of Mary Jones* on Friday evening and closing with *The Night Season* at a Sunday matinee, the Smithsonian presented the plays in their correct chronological order and as a single event for the first time. The response of this audience was especially heartening: "I very much felt the power of the cumulative experience," Ken Yellis wrote; "fine as each of the parts was, the whole was much greater than their sum."

Among the Smithsonian's audience were several visitors from Savannah who went home determined to bring the plays to their city. Soon thereafter the Georgia Historical Society agreed that this cycle belonged in Savannah, the modern city nearest the Joneses' lands and one conscious of both its rich theatrical past and its distinctive Southern heritage. By early 1985 Myers "was happy to announce that a fifth play, *The Courtship of Carrie Davis,* detailing the romance of Joseph Jones and Caroline S. Davis in 1859, had now brought the cycle to completion." Thus, when Savannah's civic celebration opened in October 1985, the complete five-play cycle could be produced for the first time.

The artistic problems to be confronted in successfully staging this cycle were—and are—considerable. Both the nature of the dramatic material and the expectations of contemporary theatre audiences compel a most careful theatrical treatment. For example, throughout the five plays Myers sought to capture the epic sweep of the letters, yet he restricted himself to the words of the letters: "Every line uttered consist[s] exclusively of words penned by letter writers more than a century ago.... One cannot, I think, overstate the advantage gained by confining the plays to the actual words of the historical persons represented on stage. Immediacy is assured: truth rings in every line." But this decision, however admirable in terms of historical and poetic truth, leaves the theatre artist to answer a difficult question: How underscore the plays' issues in the immediacy of the theatre, when the texts consist solely of the words of characters who did not themselves understand their roles in the great national drama playing out around them? The staging adopted in Savannah proposed one set of imaginative answers to the question. Because these answers may serve to guide others interested in attempting this challenging cycle, they are described here in some detail, again from *Theatre Journal:*

Southern Poets Theatre of Atlanta suggested the epic quality of the cycle by carefully selecting and ordering the sounds and sights of each play so that its relation to the whole was both clear and telling.

The sets for all plays were suitably sparse, with platforms, like medieval *sedes,* defining special playing places amidst a generalized acting area. Except for fragmentary windows and cut-out trees silhouetted against a cyclorama, the scenic environments depended entirely on the careful manipulation of lighting, sound, costumes, and properties.

In each instance the designers managed to evoke the private world of the characters and, at the same time, to underscore the larger issues of the cycle. The live music that introduced each play and reappeared incidentally within it (devised and often performed by Jay Aiken) both captured and commented ironically on the characters' innocence, their blindness to the vortex of war into which they were being so inexorably drawn. The delicate pastel, white, and floral dresses of the early plays darkened first to blues and lavenders and finally to mourning black, the careful work of designer Judy Winograd. The cyclorama, so hopeful in its blues and pinks in the early plays, captured the lengthening days of the characters and their society through harsh yellows and oranges that in turn gave way to a deep red for the final play, set within the savagery of the Civil War.

Carefully selected properties (by Alvin W. Neely, Jr.) followed family members from play to play and helped underscore one of the plays' major themes—the continuity of family in the face of the uncertainties of individuals' lives. Thus, for example, the couch around which Mary and Charles Colcock Jones conducted their courtship in the first play (described by a fellow playgoer as an elaborate storklike dance) reappeared finally in the last as a vacant monument to the dead husband and a mute reminder of the utter disruption of her life: the chaotic conditions of war prevent her sending it on to her daughter.

One important effect of the decision to reduce the number of visual details in this production was to vest each remaining detail with increased significance. But also the Spartan simplicity of the setting thrust attention firmly to the speaking actors—and so to the plays' language and ideas, where the playwright clearly intended it.

Future productions will probably decide to adopt similar strategies, but they should do so realizing that this approach requires uncommon skill—and more than a little charisma—from the performers. The actor playing Mary Jones, in particular, needs both strong memory and prodigious stamina, for she performs in three of the five plays, opening the cycle in a two-character piece and closing it (perhaps the next day, perhaps two days later) with its most powerful monodrama. Her technique must be sufficient to portray convincingly three different ages and, in the last play, to compel the attention of an audience for two hours without the support of another person on stage. Her early performance must be engaging enough to involve the audience in the simple pleasures of young love, while her final performance must be powerful enough to provide a fitting conclusion to the whole cycle.

For situations in which a five-play cycle seems too ambitious, producers might consider staging the plays singly or in less taxing combinations. For example, pairing the two courtship plays allows provocative comparisons, not only of changes in courting rituals but also of changes in the society against which these rituals unfold; or, alternatively, pairing the first and second plays offers a charming counterpoint of two generations—father and son—at Princeton; or, again, a trilogy of *The Courtship of Mary Jones, Voices of Pride,* and *The Night Season* tells the story of the cycle's central character and offers a stunning opportunity for a bravura performance. Of whatever number and in whatever combination, however, the plays of this cycle will command the most imaginative efforts of their producers, for their challenge is great.

Finally, because plays exist on a stage in front of live spectators, theatre artists must inevitably grapple with the problems of audience as well as those of text and performance. In this regard as well, *Quintet* commands careful attention. Despite the recent success of pieces like Jerome Kilty's *Dear Liar* and William Gibson's *John and Abigail,* plays constructed from letters are forever threatening to become readings rather than dramas, to substitute words for action. Moreover, it is notoriously difficult to sustain theatrical vitality in a one- or two-person play, notwithstanding Lily Tomlin's triumph in *The Search for Signs of Intelligent Life....* And in today's theatre, shaped as it is by the tempos of television, play cycles are rarely included in the repertory. Neither Aeschylus's *Oresteia* nor any of the several cycles from the Middle Ages nor Eugene O'Neill's *Mourning Becomes Electra* finds regular production; indeed, such works have all but disappeared outside of books and libraries—and this despite their acknowledged excellence. Where, then, to find a theatrical audience for a five-play cycle drawn from letters and comprising mostly one- and two-character pieces?

Quintet's own history probably offers the best answer to this question. It is not accidental, I think, that the early plays found readings in literary clubs, historical societies, universities, and on government-subsidized radio. It is equally unsurprising that the plays' early productions were at the Trapier Theatre (a small semiprofessional art theatre loosely associated with the Washington Cathedral) or that the four- and five-play cycles were first staged as commemorations, events where a special community celebrates a shared past and a current interest. Each such venue attracts people interested in language, history, ideas, and art; each draws people who agree to participate imaginatively in a worthwhile, intellectually stimulating project; and each promises something outside of—beyond—daily experience. Such is the promise of *Quintet,* and such is the nature of its theatrical audience.

But *Quintet* has another audience as well—a reading public. Readers interested in the history and culture of the Old South around the time of the Civil War or in the traditions from which the New South arose will discover in these plays a treasure of fascinating detail. Because Myers has retained the actual words of the letters, the plays reward careful reading as documents of history; because Myers has selected and arranged the letters so carefully, the plays offer an unusually concentrated presentation of history and so give the reader an uncommon opportunity to browse through the life of another time; and finally because Myers has cast the letters in the dramatic mode, the plays enliven events by engaging readers directly with the people participating in them. All those who read and enjoyed *The Children of Pride* and *A Georgian at Princeton* will want to continue their friendship with the Joneses of Liberty County through *Quintet*. Those who have not yet met the Joneses will find *Quintet* a splendid introduction to them and their world.

Thus it is probable that the future of this cycle, like its past, will not unfold in commercial theatres. Rather it will rest among intelligent readers and among the small, select audiences drawn to today's historical societies and literary clubs, civic festivals and art theatres where the challenge of text, production, and audience can be joined.

And if the challenge is great, so is the reward. These very special plays for very special audiences recapture what America's commercial theatre seems to have lost—a sense of the art as an important expression of the life of the community. They offer their reading public a window through which to glimpse living history. *Quintet* therefore deserves our respectful attention.

For information on the cycle's history, I am indebted to Robert Manson Myers and to *Arts and Humanities: A Magazine of the Liberal Arts,* a collegiate publication of the College of Arts and Humanities at the University of Maryland (Fall 1985): 2–7. For permission to quote from *Theatre Journal,* 38, 2 (May 1986): 221–24, I thank The Johns Hopkins University Press.

QUINTET

The Courtship of Mary Jones

The Courtship of Mary Jones is drawn exclusively from the letters of Charles Colcock Jones (1804–1863) and Mary Jones (1808–1869), written from 1829 to 1830, and now preserved in the library of Tulane University (New Orleans).

CHARLES COLCOCK JONES, *an attractive, intelligent young man in his twenties*

MARY JONES, *an attractive, intelligent young woman in her early twenties*

The scene is set in Princeton, New Jersey, and coastal Georgia (Savannah and nearby Liberty County) from 1829 to 1830.

Act One

As the stage lights come up, CHARLES COLCOCK JONES *enters, takes off his coat, sits at a desk, and commences writing.*

CHARLES: Believing, my dear Mary, that you, like myself, are today brooding in a melancholy way over our separation, and wishing to relieve both of us, I have pulled off my coat in Mr. King's counting room and set down to write you a few lines. . . . After bidding you a last farewell yesterday, I had a most uninteresting journey to Savannah—when awake, troubled with the reflection that I had left you for a great while, perhaps forever; when asleep, dreaming of the happy scenes just passed through. . . . I *feel* separation now more than ever before. But is there not more reason that I should? My better half is left behind. I am no more a solitary in the world. There is now one whose affections follow me wherever I go. . . . Duty requires that I should not see your face for some time. But we can pour out our hearts to each other in our letters. We can be companions, although the ocean rolls between us. And how delightful is the anticipation that your letters will be frequent and will be long! Remember—you write to him who has given you his undivided affections, and who expects the same.

MARY: In resuming my pen to address my dearest Cousin Charles I cannot but pause to reflect how new, how changed, are all my feelings since last I wrote him. *Then* the ties of relationship made it a *duty; now* affection the most sacred claims it as her highest privilege. . . . Here we are once more at the old Retreat. I have just completed the arrangement of my little quiet room, and here I seat myself at my desk by the window to write you—every object around, even to my very geranium, reviving many a pleasing remembrance. These silent walls, had they a tongue, could perhaps more truly tell my real feelings than any other object. Here restraint was ever banished. There is no earthly spot I love more than my own little garret room.

CHARLES: I came on board the brig *Francis* last evening at seven o'clock. We dropped down the river during the night; and at daylight, the wind baffling and hauling ahead, Captain Croft let go his anchor and waited for the ebb tide.... I sat on the cotton bags and looked up at the sails swelling out with the wind, and then far up into the blue sky without a cloud. Schools of flying fish, startled by the vessel, rose and skimmed over the waves on their silver wings without dipping. Oh, Mary, how often did I wish you to enjoy with me this beautiful afternoon!... After reading an hour I lay down, with the ocean rolling its waves towards Georgia, and sung "Home, Sweet Home." Oh, the long, long time before we shall embrace each other!... Do write me a long letter. Tell me your feelings since we separated.

MARY: Dare I tell you? No, not even you shall know. I sometimes feel very melancholy at the prospect of our never meeting again.

CHARLES: *You* lose but *one: I* lose *all* —and you dearer than all.

MARY: It is true I am surrounded by those who are very dear. But what now to me are a thousand friends if amongst them I do not meet my own Cousin Charles?

CHARLES: Did I show you my note to Father on the subject of addressing you? It was penned in haste on May 19th, 1829, the evening of which day we united our hearts; I shall never forget "the scene of the sofa." (*He reads.*)

"My dear uncle, I can no longer conceal from you what perhaps you have discovered—namely, my attachment to Cousin Mary. You may be surprised that I entertain more than ought to exist between those so nearly connected by blood relationship, but it is nevertheless true. I was attached to her previous to my residence at the North, and I beg that you will permit me to pay my addresses to her. You have always, my dear uncle, exercised over me the supervision of a father in all my affairs; and in this matter, as still holding this relation, I look up to you for your candid feelings and for your direction. I know the family connection between Cousin Mary and myself renders our situation delicate. It is nearer than I ever expected to approach in any matrimonial relation. I therefore need your advice. Your affectionate nephew, Charles Colcock Jones."

You know I did not insist on seeing your note to him, but left it to you whether I should or not. But his answer you must not forget to send.

MARY: Well, here it is. (*She reads.*)

"My dear daughter, I have perused your note on the important subject, and can assure you it meets with my cordial approbation. 'Tis true that I have repeatedly said that cousins ought not to marry; yet this kind of objection ought not with a parent to be insuperable. You and Charles are both old enough to judge correctly in these matters, and both members of the same church.

"Should it please God to have you at some future and suitable period united in the holy bands of matrimony, your happiness will much depend upon a reciprocity of temper in yielding to each other's weakness; for poor human nature will be frail and subject to err, and when this is the case, I hope from the discretion and good sense you both possess, proper allowances will be made.

"Wishing you all the happiness, both temporal and spiritual, that you can desire, I am your ever affectionate father, Joseph Jones."

CHARLES: Father appears to be perfectly satisfied. Does he ever say anything to you about me?

MARY: Oh, indeed he often *commences* to talk of "Parson Jones," as he is pleased to call you. But he is so inclined to be mischievous that I can never wait to hear his story out.

CHARLES: It is a splendid evening. The sun has just fallen below a cloud discharging itself in a thin shower, and the whole western horizon is a sheet of golden light, which, reflected in the ocean, bronzes its waves. The fleecy clouds next the azure are burnished gold; those resting where the sky and waters meet are fringed with silver; and above all in the blue expanse rises the crescent moon. Oh, how I love to gaze on the evening sky and watch the glow of its various dyes! Who can paint like God? . . . These are the moments I fain would have my Mary with me.

MARY: Dear Cousin Charles, how long seems the time since we parted! And how vastly longer that period which must intervene before we meet again! Still if it is to advance your interest or the interest of that sacred cause you wish to promote, I could unhesitatingly submit to twice the time of absence.

CHARLES: This afternoon we experienced a severe storm of wind and rain. I was on deck most of the time, rendering assistance; my hands are now blistered by my labors aboard. I love to see a storm; on water the effect is very fine. I love to see the power of God so displayed. And I love to see His intelligent creatures, braving the elements in fearful commotion. There is sublimity in such a scene. . . . The storm passed away, and I gazed on the red clouds and thought of the friends I had left. Captain Croft entered into conversation, and said that he had been a married man twenty-one years, and during this time his affection for his wife had increased, and he would recommend every young man to marry at twenty-one as he did. (Excuse me, dear girl, but you see verified the old proverb: "A man will speak much of that which is uppermost in his mind.")

MARY: I had a beautiful little pet given me a few days since: a young fawn about four weeks old. It is now perfectly gentle, and knows me so well that it is my companion in all my walks. So you may think of me sometimes as racing through the woods with Willie at my heels.

CHARLES: You may direct your letters to Princeton: "Mr. Charles Colcock Jones, Theological Seminary, Princeton, New Jersey." . . . And dear Mary, be good enough when you write to leave a margin as I have done, so that if our lives are spared our letters may be stitched together and afford us pleasure at a future day. . . . A thought occurs: How would my letters to my dear Mary read to a third person?

MARY: A third person? Be assured that on *my* part our correspondence shall be strictly confidential. And I am fully convinced that it will be thus with you.

CHARLES: Were I to show your letters to a third person, I should feel like a traitor, because I should betray your confiding love. Love is a miser; his treasures are hoarded for himself alone and secluded from the sight and touch of others.

MARY: Will you not, my dear cousin, destroy my letters so soon as they are read?

CHARLES: My dear Mary, you must not doubt my honor or honesty.

MARY: My dearest cousin, do not suppose for one instant that I ever doubted your "honor or honesty." Could I love you if I did?

CHARLES: I would not do anything to check the freedom of your letters, and therefore I will not suffer them to be seen by other eyes than my own.... My good friend Mrs. Mason *would* like to know something of you through *one* of them; but you will not give me permission to show her even *one*.

MARY: Your good friend Mrs. Mason....

CHARLES: Mrs. Mason is my best friend, and my only confidential friend out of the family.

MARY: At present I cannot consent to Mrs. Mason's seeing even *one*. Some twenty years to come, should God spare our lives, we will show her all.

CHARLES: I will do just as you say in this matter.

MARY: Remember—I cannot give you permission to show even *one* letter to your own Mrs. Mason. You have told me so many interesting things of her that I doubt not but I should very soon learn to love her as much as you do; but still *she must not see my letters; they are for you alone*.... And now, sir, did you not object to a third person's seeing yours? And here you want to appropriate to yourself the right of displaying all I say to you! If it would not be doing violence to my own feelings, I would retaliate upon you!

CHARLES: My dear Mary, do not fold your letters quite so hard: the paper breaks in the fold.... I shall send you by the brig a book: George Payne's *Elements of Mental and Moral Science,* just published, which I beg you to study as early as possible, for it contains that of which you stand in need every hour.

MARY: George Payne's *Elements of Mental and Moral Science.* ...

CHARLES: I send you also a stirrup, as yours is broken.

MARY: A stirrup....

CHARLES: And lastly I send you a whip—a whip—to let you know what you are to expect.

MARY: You mean to be a tyrant, do you? Well, I think your tyranny will have no precedent; for you have placed the weapon in *my* hands. And so I shall "expect"—not to fear my master overmuch.

CHARLES: Oh, you sarcastic girl! Boasting your power to rule, and shaking your scepter over my head already! I would talk *Latin* at you if I were not afraid you would guess the English of it. But *I* shall take another method of ruling you: I will unnerve your *hand* by ruling in your *heart.*

MARY: I have commenced George Payne's *Elements of Mental and Moral Science.* I study about fifteen pages a day.

CHARLES: Fifteen pages a day! Do you not attempt too long lessons?

MARY: I fear I shall make but a stupid metaphysician.

CHARLES: Dear girl, you must study well what you read. Remember—the great object in reading is not to pass over pages but to store the mind with ideas. But more of this.... We came to anchor this morning below the Philadelphia navy yard. We landed in the jolly boat, and I saw Mr. Neff in his counting room at ten o'clock. He is the same kind friend as ever. I mentioned to him *our affair.* "I suspected you, Charles," he said. "Is it your cousin?" "Yes, sir." "I thought that would be the case, from what you told me of her when you returned from Georgia after your first visit two years ago." Mr. Neff said I had been too quick, for he meant to give me a Philadelphia wife.

MARY: A Philadelphia wife!

CHARLES: Who this lady is you will know by and by.

MARY: And so, sir, you have a lady in Philadelphia as well as one in Princeton!

CHARLES: My journey is at an end. I arrived in Princeton yesterday afternoon. My time today has been occupied in unpacking my books and arranging them on my shelves, putting my room to rights, washing my desk and bookcase, attending a lecture on *faith,* and saying "Howdy do! Glad to see you! How have you been?" It is now 5 p.m.—the first leisure moment I have had today. You have my first leisure, my first communication, written with my first pen from a new quill, dipped in new ink out of a new inkstand, on the first sheet of letter paper from a new quire.

MARY: Your first communication....

CHARLES: I found my friends Mr. and Mrs. Mason at tea. They were both surprised to learn that I was engaged. Said Mrs. Mason: "I do not understand you." Said Mr. Mason: "Is it possible?" They both expressed themselves gratified; Mrs. Mason had formed a very favorable opinion of you from one of your letters to me which I showed her a year ago.

MARY: Showed her a year ago?

CHARLES: My dear Mary, she is a most charming woman, and I should be delighted to have you know her and spend some few days in her family to see her conduct as one of its heads. She expects—in case you come on this summer—that you will visit them.

MARY: My dearest cousin, I haven't the least idea of coming on to the North this summer.

CHARLES: I would invite you to spend your summer in Princeton, but it would not be proper; you know the world has forms, and it has a tongue.

MARY: Nothing would delight me more than to spend the summer in traveling throughout the Northern states and then in September visit Princeton. But there is not a person of my acquaintance going on, and to place myself under the charge of strangers would be truly disagreeable.

CHARLES: Perhaps some favorable opportunity may offer yet. It would be gratifying to me to have you spend a month or two with Mrs. Mason; you would there learn what sort of a wife would please me.

MARY: I assure you it would also be gratifying to *me* to become acquainted with your good friend Mrs. Mason—if for no other reason than the one you advance. But when you talk of my spending "a month or two" with her, you forget that I am an *entire stranger* to her and could not *yet* dare presume upon her friendship for you.

CHARLES: I am now very much engaged, having just entered upon my studies. Notwithstanding, you see that by catching one minute here and two or three there you have a long letter, which I think will have—or ought to have—an effect upon the length of your answer.

MARY: My dearest Cousin Charles—

CHARLES: Indeed, most of you at home tell your stories in short meter—though I will not complain.

MARY: Complain!

CHARLES: You treat me better than I deserve every way. And *your* letter was not short. But you wasted paper in a broad margin.

MARY: A broad margin!

CHARLES: It is quite unfashionable to leave broad margins nowadays.

MARY: But my dear Cousin Charles—

CHARLES: It is a proof, I think, that folks write more nowadays than formerly.

MARY: You perceive, my dear cousin, that I have left but a *narrow* margin for your *wit*.

CHARLES: The gentleman of the seminary who took your letter from the office, seeing a neat direction in a lady's hand, offered me the *postage* for it.

MARY: The postage!

CHARLES: I refused, and on opening it did not see reason to repent of my refusal, for it was worth considerable more than twenty-five cents.

MARY: My *dear* cousin!

CHARLES: One of the excellencies of your letter was its fair, legible character—an accomplishment to be lauded in man, woman, and child.

MARY: It is often said that handwriting is expressive of character.

CHARLES: If so, you have a good one—at least a character for neatness. And neatness in a lady is above all price.

MARY: Indeed.

CHARLES: I am extremely sensitive on this point, and perhaps with some reason, having living examples of the contrary in young ladies with whom it is my happiness to come in contact almost daily.

MARY: Almost daily....

CHARLES: They are either *sluts* or *ladies*—their hair in a gale of wind, their frocks thrown on to scare the crows, their shoes slipshod, their stockings about the heel.

MARY: To say nothing of the dust which lodges in the ear and neck while attending to household affairs.

CHARLES: I involuntarily think of Mr. John Wesley's remark to a young clergyman (Mr. Wesley, the founder of the Methodists): "Do not *smell above* ground."

MARY: Do not smell....

CHARLES: It is a Christian duty to keep our mortal bodies neat. We feel better, have better health and spirits, can praise God in consequence better, pay more respect to ourselves and receive more respect from others—while there is an essential influence in refining the whole character, moral and intellectual.

MARY: Your *New York Observer* we have found extremely interesting as containing an extensive fund of religious information.

CHARLES: The *Observer* is a valuable paper. I wish you could prevail on your friends to take it. We all ought to have a *thirst* for *news,* and not sit down at home and look no further than where the forests girt our fields. There is a world lying in every direction beyond that line.

MARY: Father wishes very much to take me to Savannah this winter.

CHARLES: Go by all means, and write me a long letter from Savannah. Embrace every opportunity of going beyond the immediate circle of your acquaintance.

MARY: Should we go, it will not be before January, as Father's business will detain him until that time.

CHARLES: There are no copies of *The Handel and Haydn Collection of Church Music* in town; but Mr. Mason expects some of the last and best edition (the fifth) very soon, and you will please accept a copy as a present from me. I shall request Mr. Mason to mark in the index some of the most beautiful tunes for you, and if we are spared to meet again, shall expect to sing many of them to your playing.

MARY: I must return you many thanks for the music.

CHARLES: There are a great many beautiful compositions in that collection, and the musical as well as the Christian world is greatly indebted to Mr. Mason for his labor in arranging and selecting the pieces.... I frequently wish to spend an hour with you at the piano: pianos and ladies are scarce articles in Princeton.

MARY: I shall prize *The Handel and Haydn Collection* as *your gift*.

CHARLES: My dearest Mary, I long to see you. It is now forty days since we separated. The loneliness of my feelings at times is indescribable. In the midst of society to be alone is solitude of all the most solitary.... Will you forget me? Will you forget those hours we spent—and how swiftly did they fly!—after our engagement, when we walked in the piazza at the Retreat in the stillness of evening and opened our hearts to each other? Or those hours on the sofa, when we committed ourselves to God in our union?

MARY: Oh, my dear, dear Cousin Charles, if you only knew how much I think of you, you would never even ask if "I could forget"! Did I not remember you but too well—even when I was not privileged to love you? And would it be possible that I could forget you now—you to whom I am bound by the sincerest affection of the heart; you, the only being I have ever loved? If you find no cause to doubt your own heart, you must not doubt mine.

CHARLES: Let us be careful, dear Mary, not to make gods of each other. A gentleman inquired of Professor Stuart "how much a man might love his wife." Professor Stuart replied: "A man may love his wife as much as he pleases—if he will only take care to love God supremely." Do write constantly. No ceremony should exist in *our* correspondence. You write me less frequently than you ought. Recollect I can easily pay you in your own coin.

MARY: If it is a trouble to you, if it interferes with your time or duties, then do not write; but if you can make it convenient and feel inclined, then I shall ever be delighted to hear from you; for nothing thus far but your kindness in writing me so often has in any degree ameliorated the bitter pangs attendant upon separation. If I have not written so frequently as you desire, then I will henceforth commence a reform.

CHARLES: And now shall I tell you *who* have visited Princeton within a few days? Major Bulloch and lady, Mrs. Elliott, and Miss Corinne and Miss Hetty. It was indeed strange to see Liberty County folks in Princeton. Some of them, after viewing our delightful scenery and connecting it with the hospitality of our society, observed that it would be difficult to be satisfied with Georgia again.

MARY: Such is often the *first* effect of travel. You feel home to be an inferior place. But let the novelty wear off, and you begin to grow weary and to seek for that retirement, for those conveniences, for those friends which home alone can furnish you. You begin to feel that "There is no place like home."

CHARLES: I think, however, that no person of common sense would deny, even upon the slight acquaintance of a few months, that New England is a country preferable to Georgia. Admitting that Georgia has as fine a climate and as beautiful scenery, which she certainly has not, yet the curse of slavery would give New England an incalculable superiority.

MARY: The curse of slavery....

CHARLES: Were you, my dear Mary, to reside a few months only in a *free* community, you would see more clearly than you now do the evil of slavery. There is a calmness, an order, a morality, a general sentiment of right and wrong, a justice, an equality in this society which is not to be looked for in ours.

MARY: The *principle* of slavery must be revolting to every feeling and reflective mind.

CHARLES: As to myself, I spend many an anxious thought upon the subject of slavery—the greatest evil that ever afflicted human society; a violation of all the laws of God and man at once; a complete annihilation of justice; an inhuman abuse of power.

MARY: With you I think slavery one of the greatest curses any nation should have to contend with.

CHARLES: I do not say that we are chargeable with all this in the first degree, for the evil has been entailed upon us. But I fear there is awful guilt resting on our country, because there are no steps taken to remedy the evil.

MARY: The only efficient obviation of the evil is total abolition.

CHARLES: Total abolition.

MARY: Still I do not think that it is to be done at present; and when effected it must be through the interposition of the general government, for there are not many individuals who would be willing to beggar their dependent families through such philanthropic motives. Neither do I think it would at all promote the slave's interest to liberate him in his present degraded state. He is devoid of every principle of moral rectitude, divested of all the finer sensibilities of our nature. The master's scowl or the master's rod forms the only barrier to the commission of crimes the most atrocious. I am sure I know not a dozen slaves that I could unhesitatingly say I thought capable of self-government.

CHARLES: How often do I think of the number of hands employed to furnish *me* with those conveniences of life of which *they* are in consequence deprived! How many intellects—how many *souls* perhaps—withered and blasted forever for this very purpose! Did God design this?

MARY: For myself I feel greatly dependent upon them for ease and comforts; and to me it seems a greater kindness and a more Christian act to seek to raise them first in the scale of moral excellence by treating them more as rational beings and trying to instill into them virtuous principles. I would not wish to open to them the field of science, for that would only awaken them to a sense of their own misery without in any degree advancing their happiness. I would desire for them more religious instruction: teach them to feel that they are immortal, accountable beings; teach them *whilst your slaves* the duty of obedience from Christian principle.

CHARLES: I do not wish to marry until I have some prospect of a support independent of slave labor, so that I may be left free to take that course with my own slaves which Providence may mark out. What would I not give if our family were freed from this sort of property and removed beyond its influence!... Last Sabbath, at the request of Mr. Badger, I delivered an address to his congregation on behalf of the Colonization Society. Its design is to remove from the United States the colored population, bond and free, so far as this may be made practicable, to the coast of Africa. There they will form a powerful republic, civilized and Christianized, to suppress the slave trade on the western shore and if possible on the eastern, to open an extensive trade with the nations in the interior of Africa, to send them teachers and missionaries to reclaim them from their heathenish condition. What bright hopes may we not safely entertain for the conversion of Africa—that long-neglected, long-despised, long-persecuted country! What bright hopes of the suppression of the horrible traffic, the slave trade! What bright hopes of the ultimate destruction of the system of slavery; of the rescue of nearly three million of immortal beings from ignorance and oppression and iniquity; of their establishment as a free people among the nations of the earth!

MARY: I have a request to make of my Charles—one perhaps which may rather surprise him.

CHARLES: Surprise?

MARY: You know Father's feelings towards you. He now loves

you as his own son. He has often expressed a desire to see your letters, but thus far no eye but mine has rested upon them.

CHARLES: No eye but yours....

MARY: If it meets your entire approbation, I should be pleased to show him *one*.

CHARLES: Certainly. If it is Father's wish, we ought to gratify him.

MARY: I think as our father he merits this confidence, but I wish to consult your feelings about the matter.

CHARLES: Indeed, as you intimate, it is our duty.

MARY: Remember—not all; only one.

CHARLES: You can show him as many as you please.... And will you be good enough to tell Father to send me fifty dollars as soon as this reaches you?

MARY: Fifty dollars....

CHARLES: Do not forget this, Mary. You know what a great convenience *cash* is.

MARY: Indeed.

CHARLES (*hesitating*): I am about to address my dearest Mary on a subject which I know is of a delicate nature, and may almost be considered beyond the pale of remark by the ladies.

MARY: Beyond the pale?

CHARLES: You know to what I have reference. When riding up from Sunbury the day before we parted, you observed that "my influence would never be so great over you as to make any alteration in your opinion and practice."

MARY: Oh, that was a silly speech!

CHARLES: Now, it does appear to me, Mary, that in this matter all society is in a very great error. It is among ladies what intemperance is among gentlemen. It yearly slays its thousands; and I cannot account for the universal silence respecting it except on the ground of the peculiar delicacy of the subject.

MARY: My dearest Cousin Charles—

CHARLES: My first reason for wishing you to make some reform in your habit is this. It is destructive to the beauty and vigor and health of your frame. Our dress should never be such as to prevent the free movement of our bodies and limbs in any direction. Place *me* in such limits, and you might as well shoot me.

MARY: But, Charles—

CHARLES: Not only is this destructive to your health, but it is a duty—a Christian duty—for you to be careful of that body which God has given you for wise and holy purposes. If we read the Scriptures attentively we find that our accountability for the use of our bodies is very great. Can we make ourselves more beautiful than nature has made us? Can we improve on the work of Infinite Wisdom? I do think it is your duty, dear Mary, as a Christian to consider this matter.

MARY: My dear cousin—

CHARLES: You know I love to see you dress neat, and you must not understand me to wish anything of you inconsistent with a genteel appearance. But I simply wish to ask your attention to this habit and consider if you are not indulging somewhat beyond the line of prudence.

MARY: Beyond the line of prudence?

CHARLES: I do not *say* that you are; I only fear it. Mrs. Mason uses stays, and she told me it was in obedience to the wishes of her husband; but she uses them only for the purpose of preserving her dress in a neat and genteel set.... But enough. I will not ask you to answer me on this point. You may, however, tell me you are *improving*.

MARY: I sincerely thank you for the solicitude you express on my behalf, and I trust your affectionate advice is neither unappreciated nor unheeded; and if upon your return you find I have improved, I shall only ask as my reward that you forget that silly speech. Ascribe it to girlish folly. Oh, dear Cousin Charles, you do not know in me how many, many imperfections you will have to contend with!

CHARLES: If there is anything in *me* that you would wish different, I do not think that you would hesitate to tell me of it. Believe me, dearest Mary, you can never do me a greater kindness than when you point out my faults.

MARY: I do not think myself a proper person to judge of your faults, but I will candidly say that so far as you are known to *me* there is nothing in your character that I should desire altered. Still you must not imagine that I think you perfection. Others I have heard complain that there was an occasional austerity of manner about you rather unbecoming your age and profession.

CHARLES: The fault which you mention—austerity of manner—I am sensible of. You know my natural disposition is quick and impetuous and rather overbearing. But I have acquired considerable control over my disposition, and I hope finally to acquire complete control over it. There is nothing in my eyes so unamiable as a person of a passionate temper. I had as leave be companion with a wasp or a tiger cat.

MARY: I presume by this you must have received Father's letter with the remittance of fifty dollars.

CHARLES: Tell Uncle that I have received the fifty dollars, and shall write him soon.

MARY: Today I have been sadly disappointed. The boy returned from the Boro bearing no letter from my ever dear friend. You have indeed completely spoiled me, for now if my letter comes not at the anticipated time, I am all anxiety, and immediately commence my regular routine: "What possibly could have prevented his writing? Perhaps he is not well. Perhaps he is too much engaged. Perhaps—"

CHARLES: I have just eaten a hearty Yankee dinner—a fine piece of corned beef, a piece of fat pork, fine fat chicken, cabbage, squash (like our pumpkin), potatoes, beets, bread, apple pies (tarts, as we call them), and cheese. I feel considerably refreshed. The family here are very kind. Those people who accuse Yankees of a want of hospitality do not understand the matter at all.... When the folks in this country wish you to do anything for them, they do not say: "Do this," or "Go there," but in a milder and politer way they say: "*Won't* you do this?" or "*Won't* you go there?" They express their commands by wishes. We fall into an authoritative mode of commanding, as well as of speaking, from our habit of commanding slaves.

MARY: On the 31st of last month I had the pleasure of attending the wedding of one of my friends, where I officiated as bridesmaid—Harriet Lewis to Mr. Pynchon.... The spirit of matrimony seems to be raging in our county with uncommon violence, and I hear of many weddings to be in the fall and winter. There is Miss Jeannette Thomson to Mr. Henry Stevens, and Miss Sacharissa Axson to Mr. *Moses* Jones. And what will you say to Colonel Joseph Quarterman, who having enjoyed an undisturbed bachelorship for forty years is now about to take unto himself the plague of a young wife to torment his declining days? Yes, he is positively engaged to Harriet Stevens.

CHARLES: It may surprise you to learn, knowing as you do my preference to rooming alone, that I am now located in the seminary building in a warm, well-furnished, and carpeted room with a classmate, Mr. Jonathan Trumbull Backus.

MARY: Jonathan Trumbull Backus....

CHARLES: He is a young man of property and of amiable disposition and very accommodating; we have been together three or four days, and seem to suit each other very well thus far. He was an entire stranger to me, but being anxious to obtain a good chum, he proposed the thing to me through a mutual friend. I am more comfortably fixed now than at any other time since my residence from home. A servant man, hired by chum, makes our fires before daylight, saws and fetches up our wood, and cleans our boots and shoes.... My reasons for entering into this arrangement were briefly these: to become better acquainted with my classmates; to deliver myself from seasons of low-spiritedness; to learn and correct any offensive personal habits if any existed; and to overcome a disposition to be alone which has of late very much increased on me. My social character has been suffering.

MARY: Jonathan Trumbull Backus.... Your chum has really a formidable name.

CHARLES: My chum and I rise between five and six in the

morning. I leave him to his devotions, and while all the heavenly hosts are shining I take my walk of three miles down to Kingston and return about breakfast time. These morning walks are invigorating and delightful. Sometimes the cold attacks my ears—and hands, as I wear no gloves. But between rubbing the one and swinging and clapping the other I manage to keep them comfortable.... Princeton is a great place for bad weather during the winter season. I may safely say that it has rained more than half the time since I've been here. We had a fall of snow of two or three inches last week. I have bought a pair of India-rubber shoes: Princeton is a town of mud.

MARY: Since last addressing you 1829—that most interesting period of time—has been registered with the past; and now for the ensuing 1830 allow me in sincerity to wish you a Happy New Year.

CHARLES: A Happy New Year to my dear Mary! May the choicest of Heaven's blessings rest upon you! During the year 1830 may you grow wiser and better, and consequently be happier than in any former years of your life!... My dear Mary, I would give something considerable to see you.

MARY: You cannot wish to see me more than I do to see you. It will be nine months the coming 29th of February since we parted. Have they seemed long months to you? Oh, with what fearfulness do I sometimes look forward to the nine longer still that must intervene ere we meet again!

CHARLES: I wish I had a miniature likeness of you. Do you know that Mrs. Robert McConnell has a likeness of me, in India ink, taken somewhere in 1821 or 1822?

MARY: I must really manage to rob Mrs. McConnell of your likeness. The profile you gave me more than two years ago I have kept with the greatest care, and although it is but the mere shadow of my absent friend, yet how often and with what interest have I gazed upon it!

CHARLES: How *old* are you, Mary?

MARY: How old?

CHARLES: You're not afraid to tell your age now, since you're engaged.

MARY: I'm not afraid to tell my age under any circumstances. I lack from the 24th of September to the 20th of December not quite three months of being four years younger than you are.

CHARLES: I was twenty-five the 20th of last month.

MARY: I'm too old for you, am I not? According to the present matrimonial fashions the gentleman should be at least from ten to twenty years older than the lady—or she two or three years older than the gentleman.

CHARLES: You must know that I have dissolved copartnership with chum Backus, and am now rooming about half a mile from the seminary at Mrs. Brearley's. An aged widow lady she is, in comfortable circumstances. She has three daughters living with her, who alternately for a week at a time preside at the table and attend to the domestic duties of the family.

MARY: Three daughters....

CHARLES: My room is carpeted, neatly furnished, with a large mirror and a most noble bed. And as to our *table*, it is bountifully supplied, and everything served up in genteel style. My expenses including everything excepting wood and lights is $2.25 per week.... It was an experiment with me, going into the seminary. It was pleasant at first; but even then there were many serious inconveniences. I found my chum on more intimate acquaintance not a proper associate for me, whatever he might be to other men. I could not have so perfect a disposition of my time as I wished, particularly in the matter of private devotions. Nor could I study to advantage with another person in the room. And finally my rest was uniformly broken somewhere between three and five o'clock every morning, for Backus rose in that time; and thus, as I never retired before eleven or half-past eleven or twelve, my sleep was too short for health.... Here I am once more alone; nor shall I be caught rooming with any man again.

MARY: Father made me read your letter to him, and laughed heartily at the idea of anyone's walking forty miles just for exercise.

CHARLES: Father may laugh as heartily as he pleases, but I actually did walk down to Philadelphia, a distance of forty miles, just for exercise. On Tuesday February 9th I set out about eleven o'clock from Princeton, dined at Trenton, and arrived at Bristol a little before sundown, twenty miles from Princeton. I wish you could witness the winter scene which lay around me in this walk. The snow covered hill and valley, and wrapped nature in her winding sheet. The Delaware was frozen, and lay in its long reaches a field of snow and ice.... After an excellent supper, feeling a little fatigued, I retired, but slept badly; in addition to the excitement of overfatigue I was disturbed by the continual tramp of horses and jingle of sleigh bells. I set off in the morning after eating a piece of bread. I breakfasted on the road; and the landlord, taking me for some straggler, set me down at table with some wagoners. He only charged me twenty-five cents, however; and perhaps I gained something for keeping such company.... I reached Mr. Neff's counting room at half-past seven. He appeared glad to see me, and was surprised at my walking down.... I returned on Saturday the 13th to Princeton. The conversation in the stage turning on the subject of slavery, after expressing my views of it a young man from Virginia, addressing me, said: "You *Yankees* always express a great deal of feeling on this subject." He opened his eyes and stared, and the laugh of the stage was turned on him, when I declared myself a Georgian—farther south than he. I can pass very well for a Yankee, you perceive. How do you like the idea of marrying a *Yankee*?

MARY: I have had many invitations to spend some time in Savannah, but rather think at present I shall not avail myself of my friends' kindness. City life fritters away one's time without leaving any pleasing review to mark its flight.

CHARLES: If you go to Savannah, remember that time is precious, and that such visits are apt to dissipate holy feeling.... During the past month I have formed a "Society of Inquiry Concerning Africans." I drew up the constitution and bylaws, and was elected president. The design of the society is to collect information respecting the condition and prospects of enslaved and manumitted Africans throughout the world, but more particularly those of our own country; to collect information respecting all benevolent societies designed to meliorate the condition of this neglected and degraded portion of the human family, and this with the view of ascertaining our personal duties and responsibilities towards them, and the manner in which their best interests may be promoted.... I am in hopes that the society will be productive of much good. I am to deliver the first address before it shortly after the recess.... You, my beloved girl, know that my feelings are much interested for the poor Africans. I have many painful struggles, and cannot discover so plainly as I could wish the path of duty. I hope your feelings are not different from mine. We *may* be called to take some decisive steps with regard to these immortal beings over whom God in His mysterious providence has placed us.

MARY: I returned from Savannah yesterday after an absence of more than a month. The change from town to country at this season of the year is most agreeable. The air is so elastic, so bracing; everything seems so delightfully fresh; and nature, decked in her loveliest garb, smiles all around.

CHARLES: Am glad you are home safe again. You will now write me often. I was growing quite hungry for letters during your absence.

MARY: In Savannah I met Mr. Burroughs, late from Princeton. It was a great satisfaction to me to converse with one who had so lately been with *you;* and had I indulged my inclination, I would have made Mr. Burroughs heartily sick of me and my questions. He told me much that was extremely grateful to my ear. Indeed, you are becoming so popular, and have made so many new friends, that I am almost tempted to fear you will forget those in poor far-off Georgia.

CHARLES: You must not credit all you hear from others respecting me. Knowing our connection, it is natural for them to flatter. And you know a lover is easily flattered. Perhaps you will be sorry of your bargain when you meet a slim, pale, long, thin-visaged man—as Georgians say, "of no much account anyhow." You must expect only a plain homespun man and nothing more.

MARY: I have a large edition of Watts's Psalms, but I wished a smaller to carry about with me, and I intended procuring one when I went to Savannah; but on attending the Independent Presbyterian Church I sat in the very pew which you occupied, and when the hymn was given out someone handed me a very small hymnbook, upon a blank leaf of which I observed written "Charles Colcock Jones." So after the services were over, instead of returning it I just slipped it into my bag and walked off.

CHARLES: Your finding my little psalmbook in the Independent Presbyterian Church affected me. Trifles do this frequently. The remembrance of that little book brings to my mind many painful and some pleasant thoughts.

MARY: I have commenced reading your Bible through as I promised before your return, and find your many little marks highly interesting, for they serve measurably to convey to me your opinion of particular passages.

CHARLES: My dear Mary, do not give over diligent study. Improve your intellect as much as possible; you may never have a better opportunity than at present.... What are you studying? How do you spend your time?

MARY: In the morning I always aim to rise with the sun, and after certain necessary duties of the toilette I devote the remainder of my time until breakfast to reading my Bible. After this I usually devote about two hours to Payne's *Elements of Mental and Moral Science.* In the afternoon I read some religious biography, some pious work, or anything interesting I can come across. Sometimes I write letters, though that is most generally reserved for my night's work after all the folks are quietly asleep.... My time, I hope, is not altogether unimproved; I have my books, my piano, my work, my morning rides, my evening walks.

CHARLES: You certainly ought to be reading some history. What histories have you read?

MARY: Very few indeed—merely those most generally used in schools. Whilst in Savannah I purchased Irving's abridged *Life of Columbus,* which I shall read shortly.

CHARLES: If you wish to try the powers of your mind, you may read Foster's *Essays* and Butler's *Analogy;* they are among the books I sent home lately.

MARY: As you request particularly that I read Foster's *Essays* and Butler's *Analogy,* I will ask Cousin Susan to lend them to me; but I should not have done it otherwise, as they were never offered me, and I do not like to *beg*.

CHARLES: You "do not like to *beg*"! Beg what? Ask *my sister* to lend *you* books that belong to *me*? My dear Mary, let me speak plainly. I never wish to see you, as long as I live, exhibit such nicety, such overexactness, in your intercourse with any friend, much less a sister. I have an utter disgust to all such littleness of pride. It is not true and proper pride; it is the lowest sort of pride. Build your character on a broad foundation of benevolence; aim at a character that is full of love, that is humble and meek, that will attract the love of others. There are great souls and there are small souls. I want my dear Mary to be a woman of a great soul.

MARY: I am truly sorry you put so serious and unpleasant a construction upon my remark about your books. The manner in which I expressed myself I grant was unfortunate, but whatever my *words,* I know my *feelings* were not that I felt too proud to ask your sister to lend me books which you desired me to read.

CHARLES: Forgive me, my dear Mary. My words expressed more than I felt in your case; affection made them strong.

MARY: Next to *your* confidence and affection and that of my own father I am sure I wish to gain that of your sisters; and I hope that no attentions on my part shall ever be wanting to secure it.

CHARLES: I know your natural dispositions are free and open and generous. I know, too, that you love my sisters; nor do I fear that you will do everything on your part to conciliate their affections.... You must let me scold you sometimes; if I were not jealous over you with the jealousy of love, I should not attempt such a thing.

MARY: I have been very much interested today with Mrs. Cary's *Letters on Female Character,* and so far as I have progressed—

CHARLES: "Progressed"! You use *progress* as a *verb*. There is no such verb in our language.

MARY: No such verb in our language?

CHARLES: I am aware that it is sanctioned by some good writers of the present day, and you may be one of them; but I beg leave to protest against its use.

MARY: For the correction of my faults I shall ever thank you, and esteem it one amongst the greatest displays of your affection. Your criticism is, I know, a received one amongst the literati of our land.... As I was about to say, so far as I have *progressed* in Mrs. Cary's *Letters on Female Character* I think it a work of considerable utility—particularly so to Southern females. Mrs. Cary is a native of Virginia, and thus her knowledge and information respecting our slaves and domestics is all practical and thus rendered doubly valuable.

CHARLES: Amidst all your pursuits do not forget to pay some attention to the *practical* duties that may devolve on you by and by. I refer to domestic economy, housewifery, etc. It is very probable that we shall want something to eat after we are married.... My remark suggests one thing: The kind ladies with whom I board know nothing about the preparation of corn for the table; and it has been so long since I have attended to cooking that I am wholly unable to give them any useful information in the matter. I therefore request you as soon as possible to send me a receipt for preparing and boiling hominy, for making corn loaf bread, corn journey cake (or to speak plain English, johnnycake), rice loaf bread, and hard bread. I say "as soon as possible," for we shall have no food in the shape of corn until the receipts come.

MARY: Well, I shall make but a poor cook, and I expect to receive many a scolding from my master for inattention and forgetfulness, to say not a word of indolence, one of my besetting sins.... For boiling hominy: Take one quart of fine grits, and after having washed it in two or three waters put it in a pot containing about two quarts of water and boil it until well done.... For corn loaf bread: One pint of very fine flour, one teacup of milk, one egg, and a small lump of butter, beaten well together, forming a thick batter, then poured into a pan or small oven and baked.

CHARLES: Thanks for the receipts; I shall hand them to the Miss Brearleys tomorrow morning.

MARY: I was afraid to send you all at once lest I should have nothing interesting to conclude my next letter with.

CHARLES: Mrs. Brearley has given us corn bread very frequently, made after your receipt, and it has been very excellent. She was surprised that so good bread could be made in so short a time and in so simple a manner. *Corn* is very little used on table in this country. You must send the other receipts.

MARY: Here they are. For rice loaf bread: Take one quart of rice. Wash it well. Then beat it very fine. After sifting there will be about half a pint of the coarse broken rice remaining; take this and boil it until completely done. When nearly cold mix your leaven with it; then add the flour; put it in a pan by the fire or in the sun, and when fully risen bake it.... For johnnycake: One pint of flour, a little milk, a little lard. When mixed bake upon a board. Hard bread is made by taking out the inner and soft part of the johnnycake and then turning the inside next the fire.... I have been housekeeper for the last three weeks, so this will account for the *great knowledge* I have exhibited in this necessary part of a woman's education. But I cannot say that my partiality for it increases the farther I dive into its mysteries.

CHARLES: So you don't like housekeeping! What will you do by and by when most of the temporal cares of this sort must come upon you? You must learn to be a good housekeeper. I love to see order, dispatch, neatness about a house, and everything conducted without hurry and noise.... If all things were ready, I should be glad if we could go to housekeeping tomorrow. Would this be too soon for my dear girl?

MARY: How did you succeed in your address before the Society of Inquiry Concerning Africans?

CHARLES: So far as I could judge, it gave very general satisfaction. The design of my address was to show the duty and necessity of establishing missions to the slave population of the United States. There were twenty or more ladies of Princeton present, together with the professors' families, clergymen, and a part of the board of directors of the seminary.... Afterwards Mr. Russell thanked me for the hints I had given him on Southern missions; said he wished me to carry my plan into execution; said the Board of Missions would do anything in reason to assist me.... Yesterday Dr. Miller accosted me: "Mr. Jones, why do you not always speak in that warm, animated manner that you did on Friday night?" I answered that I always did when I had an object to accomplish, but in the oratory (where we deliver our sermons before the class for criticism) I could not well do it, for there was nothing to excite me. "Well," said he, "cultivate that warm, animated delivery and that pointed manner of expressing your thoughts, and you will make an impressive speaker." He asked me if they would not *excommunicate* me in Georgia!

In addition to this I have prepared my presbyterial exercises—one, you know, in Latin! Your dear friend is no scholar; it is hard work for him to use his own mother tongue with decency, much more for him to write in an unknown tongue—a language that cost me more labor to acquire than both Greek and Hebrew *twice* over.... But it is all finished now. Will you believe it—I am licensed to preach the everlasting gospel of our Lord and Saviour Jesus Christ! The Presbytery of New Brunswick met at Allentown, about fifteen miles from this place, on the 27th of April. Six of us went down. My license is dated April 28th, 1830, Allentown, New Jersey.

MARY: So you are really licensed to preach!

CHARLES: It will be five years the 10th of this month since I commenced my studies for the ministry.

MARY: I must really congratulate you upon your successful examination.

CHARLES: The Rev. Mr. Jones, a settled minister in New Brunswick, asked me to come down and preach for him on the coming Sabbath. His brother-in-law in Princeton furnished me with a horse and sulky, and I drove down to New Brunswick on Saturday afternoon and preached on Sabbath afternoon to a full congregation my *first* regular sermon—and the *first* Sabbath after my license. Oh, Mary, it is a solemn thing to preach the gospel to immortal men! I never had such feelings before. The *authorized* manner in which I appeared before the people affected me.... I assure you the course of my future life as a minister of the gospel is wholly undecided. It is not certain that I shall make Georgia my home.

MARY: Not certain?

CHARLES: You know that I have always been deeply interested for the colored population in slavery in the United States. It has long been a doubt in my mind whether I ought to return to Georgia and endeavor to do what I can for them there as God shall give me opportunity, or devote myself at once to them in some special efforts in connection with the Colonization Society. Which way the scale will turn, I do not know. It is high time that our country was taking measures of some sort toward the ultimate emancipation of nearly three millions of men, women, and children who are held in the grossest bondage, and with the highest injustice.

MARY: But where are the men to devise and execute such measures?

CHARLES: Nowhere. The whole country is dead on the subject, while a vast amount of passion and prejudice and self-interest and difficulty is set in opposition to every attempt to bring it forward. But matters cannot remain as they are. Some movement must take place.... I am, moreover, undecided whether I ought to continue to *hold* slaves. As to the *principle* of slavery, it is wrong! It is unjust, contrary to nature and religion, to hold men enslaved. But the question is: In my present circumstances, with the evil on my hands entailed from my father, would the general interests of the slaves be promoted best by emancipation? Could I do more for the ultimate good of the slave population by holding or emancipating what I own?

Last week I strolled into a book auction room and lighted on a small volume of letters written by a lady from the island of Santo Domingo during the period of the insurrection. It was entitled *The Secret Horrors of Santo Domingo*. I read the volume through standing at the shelf from which I took it.... To illustrate the ferocity and perfidy of depraved and unrestrained ignorance fired by passion, I offer you the following from the book. Count Rochambeau with his French troops was obliged to capitulate when he evacuated the town. The Negroes encouraged all the whites to remain—with the hope of protection and security. Many remained. Their repose was transient; in a few days the Negroes collected and slaughtered the males, and those who secreted themselves were hunted down and cruelly slain. The females were ravished, or driven into the streets, stripped of their finery, denied a decent dress, and forced by the scourge to bear cannonballs upon their heads a distance of two or three miles, exposed to the beatings of a tropical sun.... A colored chief acquainted with a widow lady who had two beautiful daughters encouraged her to remain on the evacuation of the town, promising every protection. She remained. After the entry of the colored troops he called upon her and proposed himself in marriage to her eldest daughter, then present with her younger sister. They instinctively shrank into their mother's arms. She replied, with that fortitude so peculiar to woman in hours of severest trial, that "death to her and to her daughters would be preferable." "You shall have your choice," he replied, and calling for his guards, commanded the mother and younger daughter to be hung immediately. After taking the elder daughter home with him, and being rejected in his suit to her, he ordered her to be suspended by the throat from an iron hook in the marketplace, where she slowly expired.... Such are some of the dreadful results of slavery. No man can predict the lengths to which exasperated, degraded men will proceed when a turn of fortune brings their former masters to petition for their mercy. May Heaven in *its* mercy never permit such scenes in our country!

FADEOUT

Act Two

As the stage lights come up, MARY JONES *is seated at a desk, reading a letter. Suddenly in a fit of pique she tears it up.*

MARY: Your letter from Princeton lies before me. I have just finished rereading its contents, and with Mrs. Mason I am almost tempted to exclaim: "I do not understand you."

CHARLES: My dear Mary—

MARY: I am happy to learn you have such "fine times." This account of Miss B. (for you have not ventured to trust me with her whole name) is something new. She must indeed be a charmer.

CHARLES: Mary—

MARY: What do you mean, "A match was brewing"? You say "I had need be solicitous"—of what?

CHARLES: My dear Mary, how *could* you speak so seriously about a matter which from my very wording you must have understood was the indulgence of a little humor only?

MARY: I must confess for a moment you startled me. Indeed, I cannot *yet* quite determine your meaning.

CHARLES: You must know, my dearest Mary, that I love you more than any other woman. How could you suffer so trifling a thing to occasion even the shadow of a doubt?... But it is doing violence to my feelings—I am sure it is doing violence to your own—to dwell any longer on this matter. Let us dismiss it. You know that my heart is "unalterably yours."

MARY: We have just had a most interesting three days' meeting at Midway Church. During the period of the meeting we had the two Mr. Pratts with us. Whilst seated with Mr. Nat Pratt he turned around and with a perfectly innocent face said: "Miss Mary, I saw your cousin in Princeton. He wishes once more to get upon the *warm side* of the earth." I bowed, and *tried* to ask him many questions. Have you ever seen his brother Horace? He is indeed all elegance. This was my first acquaintance with *him,* but before we separated we became quite sociable. Indeed, you had best not write me too much of your Miss B., lest through a spirit of retaliation I might become "greatly interested" in some elegant one.... But no, no, my dearest friend; it will not do to trifle thus with each other's feelings. Affection is a delicate plant. *I am not jealous.*

CHARLES: Oh, my dear, dear Mary, you will not find it in your heart to be jealous of Miss B.! *You* are my chosen one.

MARY: Dear Cousin Charles, how much *even now* am I dependent upon you for the happiness I enjoy!

CHARLES: And I am the same dependent creature upon you. You have taken away my heart.

MARY: Perhaps I should not confess it, but nothing at present has the power to *afflict* me more than your not writing.

CHARLES: When my letters are delayed, you must not scold, but remember that I have many things to attend to; and they do interfere frequently with my correspondence with you.

MARY: I *try* to reason a great deal about your many engagements; but it is all to no purpose: if my letter does not come at the expected time, I am disappointed. Our philosophy frequently deserts us when most required.

CHARLES: Oh, what a fervent lover you are!

MARY: I often wish I could just fly and take a peep at you one of these pretty moonlight nights.

CHARLES: My dearest Mary, if you have been thinking much of me, I have been thinking much of you. If it would delight you to see me, it would delight me to see you. You cannot long for the time of our meeting more than I do. We must wait patiently until next fall.

MARY: Only six months more!

CHARLES: But to the lover months are years—in absence. The reason why Jacob's seven years of servitude with Laban "seemed unto him but a few days" was because Rachel was *with* him. It was the presence of "the beautiful and well-favored Rachel" that made his toil a pleasure, and converted his years into days. The sacred writer says the *years* seemed *days* to Jacob "for the love he had to Rachel." But if Jacob had been separated from Rachel, his *days* would have been *years*.

MARY: And does my dearest friend hail with pleasure the first anniversary of our engagement? To me the 19th of May comes not as a common day, but replete with the full recollection of the past; and I have devoted a few of its calm, mild, pleasant hours to a review of the rise of that cherished affection which at the lapse of a year—on *my* part—finds itself proportionably strengthened.

CHARLES: This is certainly gratifying to him who can with sincerity say the same thing. My affections have gradually fixed and strengthened themselves in you, and all that wandering of eyes and wandering of heart which formerly afflicted me in my intercourse with engaging ladies has ceased to distress me, and my heart is at rest.

MARY: I thought it would be no inappropriate way of passing a part of the day in living over again the whole scene, and in rereading the constant testimonials of your regard, which have served to cheer many a moment of gloom and in a measure shorten our *at best* long separation. I commenced with your note to Father, which struck me as being more to the *point* than any communication of the kind I had ever before read. At the bottom of this was a request that I would send you what *I* had written him upon the subject. I have often reproached myself for not complying with your request; but the simple truth of it is, I wrote Father and handed him the note, never once thinking to retain a copy of it. The substance *you* may well imagine.

CHARLES: It is now delightful spring weather. Our trees are leaving out fast. The fields are green, and the forests are vocal with birds. The farmers are plowing and putting in their crops.... At this time last spring I was enjoying the society of my beloved Mary. I remember our evening walks in the piazza, and our affectionate intercourse in your own garret room. There we spent much of our time alone; and there we embraced and separated. My thoughts often attend you there. In fact, with every part of the Retreat house you are associated: the piazza, the drawing room, the sofa.

MARY: I shall never forget "the scene of the sofa." I shall never forget our kneeling to implore God's blessing upon our future union. It seemed to me the most solemn transaction of my life.

CHARLES: I have some faint idea of going to Virginia, and will pass through Washington City. A letter of introduction from Father to his old friend Judge Berrien would be very acceptable. It would facilitate my movements in Washington.

MARY: Father is at present in Savannah. I delivered your message to him about the letter to Judge Berrien; he said it would afford him much pleasure to give you one, and he would do so when he returns.

CHARLES: Our vacation commences today; Father's letter has not arrived. I shall probably leave for Philadelphia towards the close of the week, and shall determine there whether to go on to Washington or not. Congress will be in session until the 30th of this month.

MARY: Father wrote you a few days since enclosing a letter to Judge Berrien, which you must have received ere this.

CHARLES: Friday I took my breakfast at half-past five and set out on foot for Bristol, distant twenty miles. A great difference between the scenery today and that of midwinter. The country is dressed in green and cultivated like a garden; on every side the white farmhouses with red chimneys, lighted up by the clear shining of the sun, peer through surrounding foliage. I arrived in Bristol a little before eleven. Bathed my feet in cold water and remained until three; then took the steamboat and arrived in Philadelphia at half-past five. After tea I walked up to Mr. Bird's. It may perhaps be no sin in me to tell you that Miss B. is married.

MARY: Married!

CHARLES: Miss Bird was married to a Mr. Sprogel in March—a gentleman to whom she has been engaged for a twelvemonth past.

MARY: So your Bird has flown at last!

CHARLES: Saturday I walked up Arch Street, and calling at Mr. Bird's I found to my gratification nobody at home but Mrs. Sprogel (sometime since Miss B.). She received me with considerable cordiality, and we passed an hour together, conversing principally on her marriage. She played for me on the harp, and we separated. ... To have formed a matrimonial connection with her would have been a monument of my folly. Never did I feel more forcibly than in this morning's interview that those who marry from the mere dictates of passion must be unhappy. *Sense* soon cloys. The *mind* —the *mind*—is the spring from which the purest pleasures of intimate connections must flow. What—to marry and live for that species of enjoyment which the brutes—nay, the very earthworm— possesses in equal intensity with ourselves?

MARY: What think you Miss B.'s husband would say to her "great fondness" for *you* whilst her affections stood pledged to *him*? Would he love her the more for it? Would he even think it honorable?

CHARLES: Your strain of remark on Miss B. I think is by no means becoming, and not at all warranted by the notices which I have given you of our friendship.

MARY: Had Mr. Jones acted the part that Miss Bird did, the world would have looked upon it but as the everyday lot of many an affectionate girl; but for a *lady* to be engaged to one gentleman whilst entertaining a "great fondness" for another, according to *my* ideas on such subjects (although they may be old-fashioned) amounts to little less than—what shall I say? *Perjury* is a harsh word.

CHARLES: Does friendship between a young lady and a young gentleman always imply love? Cannot a young lady entertain fondness or affection in the sense of friendship without *perjuring* herself, even while under engagement? I am afraid, Mary, you were under the influence of the star of jealousy when you made so unceremonious an attack upon my friend.

MARY: My remarks arose from the impulse of a moment, and the words expressed infinitely more than my real feelings warranted. It was wrong—wholly wrong—in me to use such, and I freely acknowledge it.

CHARLES: I knew your cooler judgment would condemn what you had said; and the particular notice which I took of your remarks was to teach you *less precipitancy* in feeling—to think before you speak.

MARY: If you have never thought or acted or spoken or written what your better feelings condemned, then you know not how to excuse the faults of others. But if you have, perhaps you may remember that "to err is human."

CHARLES: I wish you to overcome that natural excitability—irritability, shall I call it?—which will never do *you* any good or afford *me* either pleasure or profit. It is a weakness of character.

MARY: Your letter has been a profitable lesson to me in more than one respect; and although I did not know before how bitterly you can scold, still I thank you for it all, and hope you will not find me unimproved after so much trouble.

CHARLES: I am happy to learn that my letter in which I "bitterly scolded" was profitable to you in more than one respect. You, like myself, and like all other *pieces of perfection,* need an occasional *emendation.* Scold! Aye, that I can—*well* with pen and ink, but *much better* with voice and eye and gesture. You have fallen into good hands.

MARY: I believe not many girls have grown up in this world with as few to restrain and correct the improprieties of their character as I have. I shall ever be grateful to you for pointing out whatever you may conceive amiss in me, viewing it as one of the best proofs of your affection.

CHARLES: It is my prerogative as your friend to watch over you with great jealousy. I know you are happy to have me do it.... Thursday I left for Washington, and fortunately had a pleasant company in the stage, going like myself to the capital to gratify curiosity chiefly.... The road from Baltimore to Washington is quite uninteresting, passing through a poor country, and barren of improvement.... I arrived about two o'clock in Washington. After depositing my baggage at Gadsby's Hotel I called on Judge Berrien, who lives near the President's on what I believe is called "President's Square." He received me politely, and after reading Uncle's letter of introduction made several inquiries after himself and family, which I answered to the best of my knowledge. Perceiving that he did not wish to put himself to any trouble, I told him I presumed he was a man of business, and that I could take care of myself, and then bid him good morning. He promised if he had time to call at Gadsby's; whether he did or not I cannot tell, as I removed from Gadsby's immediately after dinner to the Rev. Mr. Post's, who gave me the invitation of a Christian brother to stay with him. I never saw Judge Berrien but once after my interview with him. He was walking through the rotunda in company with Mr. Secretary Van Buren. I did not speak to him, as he did not see me.

MARY: Father received a few mails since a letter from Judge Berrien, mentioning your visit and expressing his regret at not having it in his power to pay you more attention.

CHARLES: It's a very easy matter for a man to write letters of regret and apology after events have transpired.

MARY: He said it was near the close of the session, and he had much business pressing upon him.

CHARLES: I hope Father thinks Judge Berrien's letter perfectly satisfactory. I *hope* he does; it is perfectly satisfactory to me.

Friday I accompanied Mr. Post to the Capitol. He is one of the chaplains. We first went into the rotunda, which occupies the center of the building. It is circular, about 90 feet diameter; its sides rise and curving inwards terminate in a dome 140 feet from the ground in front of the Capitol. If the top of the dome were completely closed, the reverberation of sound would be great; but it escapes through side windows near the top, which is glassed. But still the sounds of numerous voices, and the tread and scraping of feet on the stone floor, and the rattling of carriages on the pavements, loudly whisper along the walls; and it seems as if invisible spirits were fanning the air with their wings and mingling their voices above you.

The Capitol embraces this immense rotunda and two wings. In the northern wing is the Senate chamber, and in the southern wing the hall of the House of Representatives. In the rear of the rotunda is the library room, one of the finest rooms in the building. From the library you walk out into a portico, the top of which is supported by stone columns fronting Pennsylvania Avenue, reaching on with its three or four rows of Lombardy poplars a mile and a quarter, at the end of which on a rising piece of ground are all the public offices and the President's large White House. From this portico you have a fine view of the city, the adjacent country, and the Potomac. The library contains between twelve and fifteen thousand volumes, deposited in alcoves and arranged according to subjects—law, politics, theology, etc.

After coming out of the library Mr. Post took me into the hall of Representatives; and indeed it is splendid. The hall is semicircular; the top terminates in a dome, and at the top of this the light is pleasantly admitted and falls immediately on the desks of the members. This dome is supported by columns of pudding stone, procured in quarries on the Potomac. You know what pudding stone is: stone formed by the cement of a variety of smaller stones. Red curtains fall from the tops of the columns and hang around the room, just reaching within a few feet of the gallery. These curtains are said to be very bad for the speakers, not being good reflectors of sound. On the square side is the speaker's seat, resembling a pulpit, and in front and below it that of the clerks, and on either side that of the reporters.

Will you be surprised to learn that many of the members use no spit box at all, but pour out their tobacco *lava* on the carpet? The members generally sit with their hats on—an old parliamentary custom. They are thrown off, however, when they address the chair. While a member is speaking, unless the discussion be of interest, you will see the members busily engaged at their desks, frequently walking about, standing around and talking, though this is out of order. It strikes you at first as a confused affair. But it cannot well be otherwise. It is impossible for them to attend to everything that is going on, for they all have their own business in hand; and it is not perhaps necessary. I was surprised to see the vehemence with which many of them spoke; they used much action—the gesture *direct* chiefly—and made no scruple to use personalities.

As soon as Mr. Post had concluded his prayer in the House of Representatives he hastened to the Senate to open that; but when we arrived there it was too late; they had proceeded to business. The chamber is of the same form with that of the Representative hall, and with the same sort of furniture. It is smaller. This body, as you may suppose, is more dignified and grave. They have very little *small* discussion and *small* business; all this is done in the House. They were chiefly engaged in the passage of bills, of which there were a great number, as is usual towards the close of the session.

After spending some time in the Senate chamber I went to the top of the rotunda. The view is extensive, for the Capitol is situated on a hill. You look down towards the north and west and command the Potomac and adjacent shores, Georgetown and the hills that skirt it, and Washington spread out over a large space. The houses, after leaving what may be called the main body of the city, are sprinkled about in little settlements. From the foot of Capitol Hill to the Potomac, a mile or more, are rich bottom lands, on which were feeding a number of cattle and horses. Turning to the east you have simply a view of that part of the city in front of the Capitol and the undulating country beyond it; and to the south, that part of Washington which is called the navy yard, from the fact that the navy yard is there, and the east branch of the Potomac. . . . Coming down, I looked through one of the windows near the top of the rotunda on the people below. The men did not appear longer than your finger; and the dogs that strayed in ran about like mice.

Washington contains about eighteen thousand inhabitants,

and seventeen or eighteen houses of public worship of various denominations—all *thinly* attended. It is a very wicked place. And many of our senators and representatives share in the dissipation. They are men of like passions with other men. I could tell you stories upon them were it proper.

Saturday after breakfast Mr. Gurley took me up to the President's. General Jackson—pardon me, President Jackson—was engaged with his cabinet, consequently invisible. We were shown into the celebrated East Room, of which you may have seen some notice in the papers, as well as some notice of the cost of its furniture. It is without controversy a splendid room—more so than any I have ever seen. Mr. Gurley was in a hurry; and having quickly satisfied my curiosity, we left the President's house.

Sabbath morning it rained. I went to Mr. Post's church, and what was my surprise after entering the pulpit to look down at my audience *sprinkled* over the church! In a little while I observed a tall old gentleman with a full head of gray hair and spectacles on coming up the aisle with a lady under his arm. He looked at me over his spectacles with an eye of considerable fire and command to know who was about to preach. I recognized him immediately as the President. He always attends Mr. Post's church whenever he comes out, and that is pretty nearly every Sabbath morning. He set on the right almost under the pulpit, and during the sermon I occasionally addressed myself to the audience on that side, and his eye was always fixed on mine. Mr. Post told me that he was one of the most attentive and apparently devout worshipers in his congregation. He left the church immediately after the service, and my view of him was very imperfect—though I liked the old gentleman's appearance very much.

Tuesday Mr. and Mrs. Neff received me in Baltimore like a brother.... Wednesday I rode out to the Baltimore & Ohio Railroad with Mr. Neff. There we took passage in a car, and started in company with three or four others, each drawn by one horse, and each containing from fifteen to twenty passengers, and moving at the rate of ten or twelve miles per hour. It was the most delightful ride I ever had. We moved as tranquilly as a barge on the smooth surface of a lake, with this difference—that there was the rumbling noise of the iron wheels on the iron rails, and a sensation like a continual jar, which is not unpleasant. We rode out to Ellicott's Mills, a distance of thirteen miles. I will tell you more of this when we meet.

In Philadelphia I saw my friend Mrs. S. (sometime since Miss B.); she is settled in her own home, in fine health, and has the *fairest prospect* of doing well in matrimonial life.

MARY: So the world goes.

CHARLES: I arrived in Princeton about two hours ago after an absence of fifteen days; I have washed and dressed and dined, and now I commence to write you.... My dear girl, there is such a frequent occurrence of the letter *I* in all my communications to you that it excites my apprehensions lest the charge of egotism will be made against me, and you become heartily sick of the egotist. Would that I were able to make my letters more interesting!

MARY: Let me entreat you never again to apologize for the dullness of your letters. You know that to me they are all that are interesting. Indeed, I am almost tempted to believe that you only mean a sly reproach to the ones I send you.

CHARLES: But my dear Mary, what is the matter? A whole month and more—six weeks—have elapsed and not a line from you. You do not keep your promises. A very serious charge! Have you nothing to say? Do you cease writing because you expect me home? Have I told you to cease writing on this account? You should wait for orders, as my masters used to tell me in the counting room. Oh, I feel so warm I could scold like a termagant! But never mind; I shall *pay* you for all this when I get home.... Perhaps my letters are too frequent.

MARY: Too "frequent"! What a word for *you* to use to *me!*

CHARLES: If so, I can reform.

MARY: Let me assure you I wish no reform. For *you* to make your letters less frequent would be to make *me* less happy.

CHARLES: It seems like an age since I was at home, and somehow you all appear to be forgetting me.

MARY: Forgetting you!

CHARLES: But if you can find time and inclination to write, you may rest assured that a letter will be very acceptable.

MARY: "Find time and inclination to write"! My dear Cousin Charles, have I not given you every proof in my power of my sincere affection for you? Have I not called myself *your own* and professed to be unalterably so? Is there—can there be—a more solemn avowal of attachment than the record of the 19th of May, 1829, faithfully attests?... But you could not—you would not— have accused me of a violation of my promises had you known the circumstance which has prevented my writing, had you known that I have been really too sick to do so. For near three weeks I was incapacitated for anything like business. I took some medicine and had to be bled—when to act the part of a delicate lady I fainted.... But I have now so entirely recovered that on the 4th I attended the wedding of one of my friends: Mary McIntosh, who was united to the Rev. Dennis Winston. They have just called to bid me farewell. They start today for Augusta. She goes amongst entire strangers; leaves kindred and home and all for *him*. And yet she is happy in doing it. Strange affection this—that leads one to desert old and tried friends and cling around a comparatively unknown object!

CHARLES: Would *you* be willing to leave the low country and go with me into the up country of Georgia? Would you leave the Retreat, your relations and friends for me? Or suppose it may in the course of providence appear that I must go to the heathen across the Atlantic or Pacific, leaving relations, friends, civilization, country, *all,* for Christ's sake; would you be willing to endure the dangers, the fatigues, the privations, the labors of a foreign mission with me? Where God shall direct me to labor in His field, which is the world, I cannot tell. My daily prayer is that He would reveal it to me. When I engaged myself to you, it was my understanding that that engagement was not to tie up my hands in the gospel ministry.

MARY: Far be it from me ever to harbor the slightest wish of the kind!

CHARLES: It was not to confine me in one place when duty called me in another.

MARY: Go where duty, where the voice of God calls you; and should I be permitted to attend you, there shall I be most happy, accounting it my highest privilege.

CHARLES: Should it ever so happen that you refuse to go with me when my Redeemer calls me to any service, you must first make up your mind to part with me.

MARY: I must tell you of a little circumstance which occurred at the wedding. Soon after the ceremony was performed, old Mr. McWhir took his seat by me, and in one of his "playhouse whispers" said in an affected consolatory tone: "Never mind, Miss Mary; he'll not be long away." I of course feigned the utmost ignorance, and did not know to whom he could possibly allude.... Our engagement, of course, is now no longer a secret. Old Mr. McWhir has spared no pains in giving it the most extensive circulation.

CHARLES: Well, let it pass. It is an old saying that "truth will out"; and we must meet it with the best face we can.

MARY: I think he is one of the busiest persons in such matters that I know of.

CHARLES: What say you to the venerable old gentleman's *tying our knot?*

MARY: Old Mr. McWhir?

CHARLES: My dear Mary, I am little versed in the etiquette of making arrangements for a marriage, and so do not know whether it falls to my lot or yours to name the precise time.

MARY: I am quite as ignorant as you.

CHARLES: If nothing happens, I should like to be married on my return home next fall, or at the beginning of winter, provided it meet your consent and the good pleasure of God.

MARY: I assure you I have no desire to defer matters one moment longer than is absolutely necessary; but should it meet your approbation, it would gratify *me* to appoint the 20th of December.

CHARLES: It is a little singular that we both should hit on the same day—the 20th of December, my birthday. I will then be twenty-six.

MARY: I should be happy to learn the supposed time of your return; our arrangements must depend upon that.

CHARLES: So far as I can now judge, you may expect me about the last of October or the first of November. But you will hear from me frequently between this and then.

MARY: Write me what your wishes are, and I will endeavor so far as I am concerned to conform to them.

CHARLES: Meanwhile it would exceedingly gratify me to learn that you are engaged in writing an essay on the duties of a wife—to herself, to her husband, to her family, to her servants, to her connections, to society, and to the church.

MARY: The duties of a wife....

CHARLES: I recollect reading an anecdote a long while ago. A man passing down a crowded street was astonished at the ease and rapidity with which the multitude going in various directions passed and repassed and crossed the track of each other. He discovered the secret in the fact that every man would *give way a little* to accommodate his neighbor, and so they passed by without coming in contact. So it strikes me that as we shall as man and wife without doubt differ in many points both in principle and practice, we may "get along" without collision if we will only on either part "give way a little." This is the dictate of common sense, of affection, and of religion.

MARY: But supposing we differ on some fundamental principle of faith or practice, and you fail to convince me of error and I fail to convince you?

CHARLES: We must agree to disagree and wait for further light. And this we may do with the most perfect harmony.

MARY: But supposing we differ on the proper course to be pursued in our common affairs of business, arrangements of pecuniary matters, residence, furniture, etc., where immediate action is necessary—what is then to be done?

CHARLES: In all governments there must be an ultimate appeal. There must be some supreme power to whose decisions we must submit. Now, in matrimony the husband is that ultimate appeal, that supreme power, so constituted by nature and nature's God. Therefore in such cases of difference as you have just mentioned, I shall expect you to submit to my judgment. In such cases it will be your duty to obey and mine to rule.

MARY: But supposing you decide wrong?

CHARLES: Then experience or the after-reasonings of my wife must convince me of it. Error in the decisions of the supreme power is the consequence of human imperfection. We must endure it sometimes, and strive always to guard against it as well as we can. But in your submission and in my ruling you are not to exhibit the temper of a broken-spirited slave, nor I that of a pitiless tyrant. Your submission will be that of an affectionate, dutiful wife, and my ruling that of an affectionate, tender husband.

MARY: This looks very well on paper, but what shall the practice be?

CHARLES: Let me ask you a question. What do you suppose the apostle meant in the following passage? Ephesians 5:22–24.... (*He reads.*) "Wives, submit yourselves unto your own husbands, as unto the Lord. For the husband is the head of the wife, even as Christ is the head of the Church.... Therefore as the Church is subject unto Christ, so let the wives be to their own husbands in everything."

MARY: This passage does not imply, I should suppose, anything like the absolute servility of a slave, but that enlightened and cheerful acquiescence which reason and religion would approve. Submission in a woman, except when exacted by the unjust requisitions of a tyrant, I believe to be her duty. But obedience and reverence when yielded to a kind husband become the willing tribute of her affection. Mrs. Cary's sentiments upon this subject and my own agree perfectly. She observes (*reading*): "If a woman really loves her husband, it will give her far more pleasure to obey him than to govern him. Warm affection finds pleasure in submission, and delicacy shrinks from sway...." For myself I do not know what kind of submission I shall yield by and by. As you know, I have been all my life pretty much my own mistress, there being no one but my father to whom I felt it a duty to submit; and his great indulgence made his requisitions of the most lenient kind. So you must not be surprised if you sometimes have to bear with the self-will of a spoiled child. At all events, you must not scold too often.... I shall never forget during one of our evening rides prior to our engagement when through a spirit of contradiction I thought a little rabbit which you had just praised for a "pretty creature" "abominably ugly." You turned to me and observed that you "should like to have the taming of a shrew." I mean to *try* and save you so much trouble.... Whether I am calculated in any respect to make you happy I really do not know. I can give you but the assurance of my sincere affection and ardent desire to please you in everything.

CHARLES: This is as much as I can demand of you; only let me see you *live up* to this profession, and we may enjoy as much happiness in our marriage state as usually falls to the lot of dying man.... Mrs. Brearley has just sent me up a slice of a fine muskmelon, and I have eaten it, and with considerable gust too. I covet your melons and peaches and nectarines. We have apples but no peaches of consequence this year. It is not a region for fruit.

MARY: We have been feasting here on blackberries. I never knew them so plentiful or so finely flavored before. I have almost entirely lived on them, eating them for breakfast, for dinner, for supper. My health is very good, although I was never thinner in my life.

CHARLES: No wonder you are thin, living so exclusively on berries. You know this will not do. You must take solid food, and meat once a day.... I met recently with some most excellent remarks in a work of Dr. Buchan addressed to females before marriage. He remarks that beauty, so much desired by the sex, cannot exist without health. Beauty is visible health. Health is the effect of good air, cheerfulness, temperance, and exercise; and *I* would add of holiness of life. He condemns all use of creams, pastes, powders, and lotions; the best means of securing a skin of healthy texture is free exposure to the open air. And in proof of this he refers us to the country milkmaid with her full rosy cheek, her smooth neck and arms, teeming with health—a perfect contrast to one of your *house plants*. Give me a rosy, bouncing girl, and I will freely resign your delicate, languishing beauties. (Excuse me if I digress occasionally.)

Says Dr. Buchan (*reading*): "Pure water may be considered a fountain of health, and its frequent use is the best means of improving the skin and strengthening the whole frame. Those who have not a bath to plunge into should wash the face, neck, hands, and feet every morning and night." You know this statement suits *me* exactly. I use cold water by the quantity. Although I have no bath to plunge in, I have a substitute. Every morning after washing my head, neck, and extremities I then rub my whole body with a wet towel.

Dr. Buchan proceeds (*reading*): "The whole dress should be loose, and as light as may be found convenient with due warmth, so as not to increase perspiration too much by its heaviness, nor to check the free circulation of the blood by its pressure." At the time Dr. Buchan wrote his book *stays* were out of fashion, and he speaks of them with the utmost abhorrence. He affirms that the effect of stays is to destroy that fullness of the chest which is the distinguishing beauty of the female person. From the use of stays mothers are disqualified for discharging one of their most sacred and interesting duties, and the defect in the chest descends from mother to daughter.

MARY: My dear Charles, let me rectify a mistaken idea which you seem to have fallen into—that of identifying the stays of modern times with those worn in the days of Dr. Buchan. I can assure you they are an altogether different article. Those formerly worn were composed throughout of strips of whalebone closely stitched together, which formed around the body a complete case and restricted every motion. Those worn at present—at least, such as I wear—are totally different.

CHARLES: My dear Mary, if you have any regard to your personal beauty, to your health and happiness, to my confidence and affection, above all to your obligations to God to use in a proper manner the body which He has given you to employ in *His* service, you must utterly renounce the use of stays.

MARY: Utterly renounce—?

CHARLES: Suffer me to speak plainly. I have written you one letter on the subject. It rejoiced me to find in your reply an intimation that it was not unheeded. But I am not yet satisfied. My dearest Mary, will you lay them aside forever for my sake?

MARY: Abandon the use of them entirely? My dear cousin, I scarce know what to reply. Something of the kind, I do assure you, is absolutely necessary in order to preserve the dress in anything of genteel order. And this assertion is confirmed by the testimony of your friend Mrs. Mason. You cannot reject it!

CHARLES: I wish to receive you perfect as you came from the hands of your Maker, and not as you come from the hands of fashion—a disfigured, spoiled, marred work.

MARY: Were I to leave off what I now wear, made as they are in the simplest manner, I should be compelled to adopt something else, which in the end would not be half so comfortable or appear half so well.

CHARLES: My dear Mary, allow me to be particular with you for the first time, and request you to give me a positive answer on this subject.

MARY: I am fully persuaded in my own mind, and I feel assured that you would be also were it possible for you to know the manner in which I use them, that they cannot do me the least shadow of injury.

CHARLES: My dear cousin, give me a positive answer!

MARY: Dearest Cousin Charles, I do most seriously assure you for your sake—as I value your affection and confidence—that I will more than ever studiously guard against wearing any part of my dress so tight as to confine or press my person in the least. It shall be my study merely to preserve my dress in a decent appearance.

CHARLES: Well, I suppose—

MARY: And now, dearest Cousin Charles, will you not permit me still to retain them on these terms?

CHARLES: Your explanation is satisfactory. You *know* my remarks were dictated by sincere affection, though with my usual plainness. This is all I ask. Your promise satisfies me.

MARY: I have written you tonight since retiring to my room. It is now twelve o'clock; so you see I can sacrifice even my darling sleep for *you*. I was anxious to return you an immediate answer, and as an opportunity offered for my sending this to the Boro tomorrow, I concluded it best to rob *Mr. Morpheus* of a few of his idle hours and devote them to you rather than wait for another mail.

CHARLES: My dear friend Mrs. Mason, remarking one day on my engagement to you, said to me: "You must *begin* as you mean to *continue* and *end.*" What multitudes have dealt out to each other endearing epithets and solemn protestations and the fullest promises, who have in a little while buried all in mutual indifference if in nothing worse!

Our term closed on the 27th of September, on which day I received my diploma with seventeen others—the largest class but one that ever graduated at the seminary.... Thus has my study of five years and a half been concluded. I have not been confined to my room during all this time by sickness for more than one or two days. My health has been remarkably good. But how little furnished am I for the great work now before me!... I have a general plan, which I purpose under God to pursue, but its success is extremely doubtful: to attempt on my return home to introduce into our county a system of religious instruction by word of mouth for our poor degraded slaves, and thus if the plan succeeds and God opens a door to me, to devote my life to missionary labors among them. This is the plan in brief. How does it strike you? You perceive at once that it will be somewhat unpopular, and may excite against me much opposition, and that I shall need great judgment and prudence.

MARY: I can hardly believe that the time for your return is so near. Shall I write again?

CHARLES: You may not write after you receive this letter, as I hope to be on my way south after the 20th or 25th.... My books are all packed. My classmates are pretty much all gone. There is something melancholy in breaking up. I have formed many attachments in the North, and perhaps will nevermore renew them. It is indeed a changing world.

MARY: The touch of fall is most perceptible in nature around: the yellow leaves, the faded grass, and I may add beautiful sunsets; for there is a richness, a splendor, in our skies during a sunset in fall perceptible at no other season.

CHARLES: I am patiently waiting a reply to my last letter to Uncle, as I cannot stir a step towards Georgia without more *cash*. He wishes me to return by the way of Charleston. A classmate is going to Charleston, his native place; and we have determined to sail in the same ship, and about the last of this month, as it would not be safe to go to Charleston sooner on account of the yellow fever, which cannot reasonably be expected to cease before the fall of frost.

MARY: I should think a visit to your friends Mr. and Mrs. Mason before you return would be very gratifying. You have so often spoken of your "dear friend Mrs. Mason" that I more and more regret never having known so estimable a character.

CHARLES: My dearest Mary, I take up my pen to write you for the last time from the North, and not without many emotions. You would have no good reason to pride yourself on the friendship of that man who after spending five years and a half in the midst of an affectionate and Christian community could leave it without a single feeling of regret, or without a single feeling of pleasure because he was leaving it to return after so long an absence to the embraces of his dearest friends.... I have taken passage in the ship *Empress,* and we hope to get to sea—wind and weather permitting—tomorrow forenoon, Saturday the 30th.... I was asking Mrs. Mason if it was customary for gentlemen to make their ladies presents—of rings and such like things—previous to marriage. She replied that Mr. Mason made her a present of a ring valued at six or eight dollars, and that it was often done, but she did not conceive it at all necessary. You know I like to have value received when I spend money, and prefer making presents of such things as in themselves are of real value; therefore after mature deliberation I determined to present you with no ring, but in the place of it with what is of far greater value, although bought with the same money—a good book: Doddridge's *Family Expositor,* complete in one quarto volume. It is now at the binder's, and will be sent on to Savannah with my other books. How do you like my decision? . . . And then in addition to this I mean to present you with something which you say you value more than anything else earthly—that is, myself. And what sort of present do you mean to make me? Yourself—with the promise that you will be a sweet-tempered, affectionate, and obedient wife? I can ask no more. . . . I delayed closing my letter until this morning—Saturday the 30th. It is a clear, delightful morning. As soon as we take breakfast I shall go down to the ship. The agent appoints ten o'clock as the hour for sailing. I can scarcely realize that the hour of my departure from these favored regions is at hand. . . . You do not know how I long to see you—more, I suspect, than you to see me.

MARY: No such thing!

CHARLES: On the receipt of this you may direct a letter to me at Charleston. Do not omit doing it.

MARY: To prove to you how dutiful, how obedient I am I seat myself today to comply with your request that I would not omit writing you to Charleston. . . . Father and Mother go down to Savannah on Tuesday to make what they esteem the necessary preparation, so far as the purchasing of articles is concerned, for a certain important event. They will probably stay the remainder of the week in town, so that should you arrive—but no: I will not write it, lest I find myself anticipating your return at some precise period. I shall *try* and not allow myself even to *think* of your return until you are actually visible.

CHARLES: The *Empress* arrived in Charleston on the afternoon of the 9th after a tedious but pleasant passage of nine days. I hope to leave in the steamboat on Tuesday next for Savannah; so that I may be expected home—if my journey proves prosperous—the latter part of next week or the beginning of the week after. . . . When I arrive at the Retreat, you must not meet me with the rest of the family. Stay in your garret room, and let us meet where we parted. After being in the family four or five minutes (you can bear the delay), you may send Phoebe down to see me, and I will ask her if I can see you in your room, and then I shall run up in a second. If we meet downstairs we shall be embarrassed, and only be matter of *gazing*. I should feel "quite put out," as the Yankees say, to meet you in public.

MARY: It would be most congenial to my own feelings to welcome you in the same spot at which we bade each other adieu—at least to feel that I was shielded from every obtrusive eye; but present circumstances seem to create a necessity for its being otherwise, and I must entreat of you the favor to meet me as we parted at the carriage. It will be enough for *me;* I could not well endure its being otherwise at that time; and *one look* will convey sufficiently to *me* all that *you* would wish expressed.

CHARLES: It is agreeable to me to meet you as you propose at the carriage or in the house with the rest of the family without any ado. It will be more in keeping with that sober character which it becomes us to possess before others.

MARY: What shall I *call* you? I want a word—a name—respectfully affectionate. I know of none that suits me exactly. I believe *Mr. Jones* will answer my purposes better than any other. But you must allow me to say *Cousin Charles* as long as I can. It seems so natural, and I love it best, because it freshens so many pleasing remembrances.

CHARLES: Our correspondence seems now drawn to a close, as in all probability this is my last letter to you before we meet after so long a separation. It has afforded me many hours of real enjoyment; I have conducted it with the utmost freedom—perhaps too much so at times for a lady of your delicacy of feeling. But I have ever relied on your affection for me, and on your good sense and judgment. You will therefore forgive wherein I have done amiss; and every fault of opinion or character which you may have detected you can mention to me at some proper time, that I may amend for the sake of my own character as a minister of Christ, and as the husband of my dutiful and affectionate Mary. Hoping in the good providence of God to see you all shortly, I remain, my dear Mary, your ever affectionate Charles.

MARY: I cannot refrain from feeling some regret, although it is exchanging a shadow for the substance, at the termination of a correspondence which to me has been so productive—I trust not only of pleasure but profit—and for which permit me once for all in the conclusion to express my gratitude. The kind reproofs, the valuable counsel, the endearing regard have all sealed my esteem and affection unalterably yours. My letters have always been dictated by the feelings of the moment at which they were written, and you know full well how faulty they have been. But forgive the errors and view them only as the simple testimonials of my regard.... And now, my very dearest friend, I must conclude, hoping to resume our intercourse in a little more than a week. Until then adieu, adieu. Be assured you possess, as ever, the sincere and unabated affection of your Mary Jones.

FADEOUT

A Georgian at Princeton

A Georgian at Princeton is drawn exclusively from the letters of Charles Colcock Jones, Jr. (1831–1893), written from 1850 to 1852, and now preserved in the libraries of the University of Georgia (Athens) and Tulane University (New Orleans).

CHARLES COLCOCK JONES, JR., *an attractive, intelligent young man of college age*

The scene is set in the room of CHARLES COLCOCK JONES, JR., in Nassau Hall, Princeton, New Jersey, from 1850 to 1852.

Act One

The room of Charles Colcock Jones, Jr., *in Nassau Hall, Princeton, 1850–1851. A window (with window seat) overlooks the campus. A desk with candle, a bed, a chest of drawers and mirror, a stove, a hat rack, a trunk, a bookcase, a cabinet, a large screen, a table, and several chairs.*

As the stage lights come up, sounds of undergraduate merriment are heard from the campus below. In a moment Charles Colcock Jones, Jr., *bounds in. He is an intelligent, good-looking young man in his nineteenth year, full of energy and lively humor, now breathless from running, with a hint of mischief in his smile. He calls.*

Joe! . . . Joe! . . . Brother Joe!
(*He hangs his hat on the rack, rushes to the window and looks out, laughs, then turns to the audience and chats confidentially.*)
The boys have tonight been raising quite a fuss. They have been trying to make a large light in the third story of Old North with candles and paper. They have been crowing and howling and blowing horns and shouting "Fire!"—and all to get Dr. Maclean to come after them. In fact, when the noise was at its loudest they were calling for him. And now they are braying like so many jackasses with heads out of their windows.
(*He leaves the window, hangs his coat on the rack.*)
Last night we heard a cry of "North College on fire!" and upon rushing with the crowd into the campus we found one of the chimneys in a large blaze. Fortunately the fire caused no injury to this time-honored building.
(*He goes to the desk.*)
On the evening of the 4th we had a general outbreak. While the

tutors were all in the refectory some forty or fifty students barricaded the third entry of Old North with boards and posts and various pieces of wood. Just as they had completed their operations and were beginning to tune up the fiddles, strike the banjos, rattle the bones, and pull the bell (the bottle having already passed freely around), who should step in their very midst but the real Dr. Johnnie! Having received an intimation of the spree, Dr. Maclean had about a half an hour previous, unseen by any, entered the room of the tutor upon the third entry, and remained there quietly, sending the tutors into the refectory, until everything was completed and the barricade perfect, when, as I have said, he stepped out and detected the party. The presence of a hawk amid a flock of partridges in a pea field was never more unexpected or more unwelcome than the appearance of the doctor; and you may well imagine the smiting of knees, the dodging into rooms, the dropping of bottles and fiddles, and the slamming of doors. Those, however, who were detected became very bold, and while Dr. Maclean was chasing others they chased him. He finally declared that he would go down if they would remove the wood, and that none of them should be reported provided they would cease operations and retire to their rooms. To this, however, they would by no means assent, and after the doctor had descended, again piled on the wood, passed the bottle around freely, danced until so drunk that they could stand up no longer, pulled the bell until perfectly tired out, then emptied a keg of tar over it and fell asleep.

(*He sits at the desk, lights the candle, takes up a pen.*)

There is certainly no sense in such sprees—much nonsense and poor pay.

(*He writes.*)

Nassau Hall, Princeton, New Jersey, Friday, August 9th, 1850.... You will perceive from the date of this letter, my very dear parents, that we have at length reached Princeton.... It is with much pleasure that I embrace a few moments to spend in converse with those of my own native land, whom God has ordained as my best friends this side the grave.... In consequence of the crowded rooms in Washington and the many circumstances conspiring to engage our attention, I did not write from Washington, and consequently will commence a brief narration of those events which transpired after leaving home.

Had a very pleasant ride from Riceboro to Savannah, with the exception of the numerous jolts, which in consequence of the construction of our conveyance were very perceptible. One of the passengers, Mr. Spalding, appeared quite fond of the regular "brown stuff," and made no bones about indulging his propensities on every occasion, so that by the time we reached Savannah he was, to use a familiar expression, "pretty well corned."

Arrived at Savannah at 5 p.m., and found all friends well.... The gasworks are now in operation, and the lights in the streets and stores and private houses exhibit a marked difference to the former dull oil lamps.... In regard to our likenesses, we went to the daguerreau rooms and sat twice. Both of the pictures were very much blurred, and we consequently did not take them. Upon our requesting the officiator to try again, he said that was as well as he could do, and refused to take another sitting. He is, I think, a man of limited abilities in his profession and withal very impertinent and coarse in his manners.

We left Savannah on Monday evening and arrived at Charleston Tuesday morning at nine o'clock. Had a delightful run, the weather being calm and the sea comparatively smooth.... We sailed for Wilmington at 3 p.m. per ship *Gladiator*. Had a prosperous passage. Although many of the passengers were sick, neither Brother nor myself suffered in the least. At night the weather was so warm in the cabin that we all went up on the upper deck, crawled into a small boat which was lying there, and thus under the open canopy of the heavens laid ourselves down to rest.... Arrived in Wilmington by breakfast.

(*He hears the sounds of undergraduates outside the window, goes to the window, looks out, laughs.*)

The little fresh escaped recitation the other day by placing a large amount of asafetida upon the stool in their recitation room.

The fumes pervaded the room to such a fearful extent that it was only at the imminent risk of one's olfactory nerves that the door even could be approached. This the fresh considered quite a feat, calling it *the* spree of the session.

(*He returns to the desk, resumes writing.*)

I recognized the features of the landscape along the Potomac, and knew Mount Vernon as soon as we came opposite. While we were passing, the bell of the steamboat was tolled—a circumstance which shows in strong light what lasting veneration the people of this country pay to the greatest of men.

(*He rises from the desk, addresses the audience.*)

At Washington we put up at the National Hotel, the finest by a great deal of any in the city.... We went to the Capitol and there witnessed one of the most interesting sights I ever beheld. There were at least three thousand little children from the public schools, each schoolteacher attending his or her appropriate scholars. After forming in the grounds of the Capitol around a stand erected for the occasion, they were addressed by the mayor of the town. Those of the scholars who had distinguished themselves at a late examination of all the schools were called by the mayor upon the stage, where they were presented with silver medals by the President, Mr. Fillmore, who did this in a manner as bland and mild as can be imagined, accompanying the presentation of the prizes with a separate encouraging word of commendation. President Fillmore is one of the finest-looking men I have ever seen; in fact, he is what would commonly be called "a remarkably handsome man."

On Friday morning we visited the Smithsonian Institute, a unique and splendid edifice, constructed principally after the Lombard style of architecture, in red freestone, obtained about twenty miles above Washington. As yet it is far from completion, although the work is progressing rapidly.

From thence we proceeded to take a view of the Monument. It will indeed be a work worthy of our country. We saw several blocks from the states set in the shaft. The material employed is white marble.

We next proceeded to the White House, where we took a view of several rooms, but saw no one except the porter, an amusing Irishman. As we were entering, our hackman, a regular son of Erin, came and peeped in at the door, upon which the porter exclaimed: "Take your nose out of the passage and let the gentlemen pass!" Whereupon the hackman, drawing himself up in a very dignified posture, asked with the utmost gravity if the President was at home, and requested the porter to let the President know that he had called. It was quite a hard cut upon our driver, for he is a man not at all deficient in the development of his olfactories.

(*He hears noise outside the window, goes to the window, looks out, laughs, returns to the desk, resumes writing.*)

Just at this moment I heard a cry of "Heads out! Fire! Fire!" and upon going to the window found quite a large blaze in the middle of the campus, the boys having set on fire certain little—unmentionables.

When we arrived at the Capitol, we found both houses in session. On going to the Senate I saw Mr. Barnwell, who immediately upon the reception of your note, Father, came out, and we entered upon an interesting conversation. It is the opinion of Mr. Barnwell that the prospect for the Union was never so dull. Mr. Clay, in consequence of his having lost the compromise bill, is very much vexed, insomuch that he will hardly speak to anyone. I saw Mr. Clay in the Senate chamber. He appears to be in very bad health, and I would not be surprised if his days were not almost numbered.

There was that day a little sharpshooting between Mr. Foote and Mr. Atchison, in which the former was entirely vanquished. Mr. Foote said that "in case the Union was dissolved they would place even the smallest of the Southern states (Carolina, for instance) in the mouth of the Mississippi, and that with her alone they could stop every vessel that floated on the Western waters." Mr. Atchison replied that "he was fully persuaded that the first freshet would sweep that little state, people and all, into the bosom of the Gulf."

(*He hears noise outside the window, goes to the window, looks out, turns to the audience.*)

The faculty have held more meetings this week than in any four or five previous. Twenty students have received walking tickets, or rather traveling passports, duly signed by the reverend judiciary. Some ten or fifteen others are in much trepidation of soul in regard to their fate, halting between two opinions—strongly inclined to remain in college, and yet almost persuaded that full permission will be granted to rusticate for a while amid the interesting sand hills of the Jersey pines.

(*He returns to the desk.*)

So much for college sprees. Let those who enter into them bear in mind that those who sow tares cannot expect to reap wheat.

(*He resumes writing.*)

I am pleased, my dear parents, to see that there is a much higher moral tone here than at the South Carolina College. Although there has been some drunkenness and swearing, still it is nothing when we regard the fearful prevalence of those vices in Columbia.

En route to Philadelphia two of the passengers lost their hats in the cars, having fallen asleep. One of them, however, waking up about the time that his hat was going, made such a noise that he terrified everyone in the car, persuaded the engineer to run back, and thus recovered it. When he returned from hunting his hat, and got upon the cars, we saluted him with a loud clapping which reminded me of college times.

I have thus, my dear parents, told you all that I have either seen or heard. As you, Mother, requested that we should communicate every circumstance, trivial though it be, I have embraced the chance.

(*He leaves the desk, hesitates briefly, coughs.*)

Now to college matters. . . . I have been examined by Dr. Maclean in Greek, Dr. Carnahan in physiology, Dr. Forsyth in Latin, Professor Hope in belles-lettres, and last but by no means least, Dr. Alexander in mathematics. My examination on all of these professors was, I believe, satisfactory.... But Dr. Alexander took us first on arithmetic, next on algebra, next on geometry, then on plane and spherical trigonometry, and finally wound me up amid the intricate mazes of differential and integral calculus. In this department I must candidly say that my preparation was not competent for this institution. In the South Carolina College very little attention is paid to plane and spherical trigonometry, and none to the calculus, either integral or differential. So that in this respect "Tekel" was my portion.

(*He returns to the desk, resumes writing.*)

It is my candid belief, my dear mother and father, that I could not do justice to my senior year if entering under these disadvantages, for such a thing as taking lessons privately in mathematics would be next to impossible: it would require all my time to learn the regular recitations, and the mathematics of the junior and senior years would be more than I could well get along with. Dr. Maclean has been very kind to Brother and myself, and advises us to join the junior and sophomore classes in preference to the senior and junior. Accordingly we have determined to attend upon the regular duties of those classes until we shall hear from you.

(*He leaves the desk.*)

We have a very good room: No. 17, North College. On the east wall of our room there are prints of balls fired by General Washington at a body of Hessians who had taken refuge in this building. In the picture gallery, which is in the opposite part of the building, there is a large frame which during the Revolution encircled a portrait of George III. A ball from the American army at the battle of Princeton pierced the wall of this building and knocked out the portrait without injuring the frame; and subsequently a likeness of General Washington was put into the identical frame.

(*He hears the blowing of horns outside the window, goes to the window, looks out.*)

It would amuse you to hear the tin horns blown in the entries every morning to arouse the sluggish sleepers. The sound is somewhat the following: *roont-a roont-a ra-a-ant-a rant-a roont,* a most unwelcome noise to one who dislikes to leave a refreshing couch. This morning Dennis, one of the Irish waiters, was tooting loudly near our door, when I suddenly sprang from bed and put an end to the pestiferous serenade.

(*He goes to the table, picks up an alarm clock, winds it.*)

We have a very good little clock with an alarm, which arouses us every morning at any hour that we desire to be waked—a watcher at all times punctual and sleepless.

(*He puts on his coat and hat as if to go out.*)

There are some pretty walks around Princeton, though I have not had much opportunity to form a correct judgment of its beauties, my walks being for exercise and not so much by way of exploring the pleasures of landscape. By early rising we have an opportunity of taking a long stroll before breakfast.

(*At the door, ready to go out, he suddenly remembers something, takes off his coat and hat, returns to the desk, takes up the pen.*)

We would be very much obliged, Father, if you would send our tuition bill for this session, as the time has arrived for paying up our dues. Say $120 apiece. We will endeavor to be as economical as possible.

(*He leaves the desk.*)

Upon invitation I took dinner with Professor McCulloh on Wednesday. Spent a very pleasant time, and found his lady and sister interesting and entertaining persons. She invited me to visit them as frequently as I could. Am struck with the freedom of intercourse here between students and professors. In the case of Dr. Maclean I think this is carried a little beyond the bounds of propriety, for the students joke him to his face about getting married and so forth.

There was quite an excitement here in college a few nights ago. A parcel of town boys were in the habit of pillaging the garden and orchard of Professor McCulloh, often approaching very near his house, and using the most obscene language in the hearing of his wife and sister. He had several times driven them off, but on Thursday night they returned in increased numbers and were even more outrageous in their conduct. Seeing that they were too numerous for him to cope with single-handed and alone, he came over to our building and requested one of the tutors, Mr. Giger, to select a few of the boys to accompany him in order to drive them off. The news of their depredations, and especially their insolent language respecting the ladies of the house, acted as an electric shock to our feelings. A parcel of us accordingly were immediately in progress to the scene; but "ere we reached the point proposed" they decided that prudence was, in their case at least, the better part of valor, and made good their retreat.

Upon retiring, we heard some pistol shots in the streets, which proved to be a fight between a few of the college students and the town boys, or "snobs," as they are here universally denominated. One of them had his hat shot from his head, and several were struck with sticks. One of the students was hit by a rock. From the continued insults and depredations committed by these men upon the premises of Professor McCulloh, it was necessary that some punishment be inflicted upon the intruders; and on this account I almost regret that we did not overtake them in the very act.

Saturday night it was rumored that the "snobs" were to make an attack upon North College as a retaliation. It appears, however, that upon second thought they abandoned the purposed design. Happy it was for them that they came to this very just conclusion, for had they entered the campus they would have met with a reception so warm that more courageous hearts than theirs would have recoiled and fled. In our part of North College there were three or four muskets loaded with fifteen slugs each, one rifle which discharges thirty-one balls a minute without any intermission, besides revolvers and clubs innumerable. So you see the affair would have doubtless proved fatal to some.... Thus terminated this noted invasion of the "snobs" of far-famed Princeton upon the courageous sons of Old Nassau.

(*He goes to the desk, resumes writing.*)

In neither of these sprees, my dear parents, were your boys engaged.

(*He dots the writing paper emphatically with a "period," turns to the audience.*)

Princeton beyond a doubt affords the finest religious and moral training of any college I have ever known. On last Sabbath (as an example) we had prayers at half-past six, prayer meeting at nine, church at eleven, Bible class at three, church in town at four, and prayer meeting again at five. At half-past seven we heard old Dr. Archibald Alexander preach in the First Presbyterian Church. His text was found in Proverbs: "My son, if sinners entice thee, consent thou not." I was so much pleased with his sermon that upon my return to my room I wrote out a skeleton of it while still fresh in my memory.

(*He hears noise outside the window, looks up, smiles, resumes writing.*)

Thus, my dear parents, is the day almost totally occupied with the public and private exercise of devotion, prayer, and praise. And in addition we have during the week a prayer meeting every evening attended by one of the professors—usually Dr. Maclean.

(*He leaves the desk.*)

Last Sabbath Dr. Maclean sent me up into the choir to help out in the singing, as there are but few who will go up. There is an organ which is played by one of the tutors, Mr. Hodge; and the singing, take it all in all, is pretty fair.

Sabbath before the last the holy ordinance of the Lord's Supper was administered in the First Presbyterian Church. We listened to our president, Dr. Carnahan, giving us a pleasant and practical sermon. His discourse, however, failed to arouse the attention of one of our tutors, who slept it through, and appeared more refreshed by his slumber than by the preaching of the Word.

I find great profit both physically and mentally from my connection with the choir. At present I am the leader of "the baser sort."

Although this is an extremely moral college, and notwithstanding the decorum with which the boys behave themselves in chapel, still there is more noise in the recitation rooms than one would have reason to expect. This morning the junior class stamped almost everyone who was called upon to recite; and at the failure of one to solve the problem proposed, a member of the class exclaimed with great emphasis: "Crane roweled!"—which quite aroused the feelings of the professor, who threatened a repetition with expulsion from the room.

(*He returns to the desk.*)

I am now hard at work in my college duties—or, as Horace would express it, *totus in illis*. We have much to do by way of attending recitations, taking notes, writing out lectures, and furnishing compositions at stated periods. It is all for the best, and I have made it a rule always to be doing something by way of improvement, and to read by snatches.... I made my first speech in Clio Hall last Friday evening—with some effect, I am told by my friends. We are confirmed Clios in every sense of the term.... I have had reason to rejoice every time I think of my entering the junior class, for lasting benefit will doubtless accrue from a two years' course at this institution.

(*He leaves the desk.*)

The class of which I am a member—the immortal junior class of 1852—is very large, numbering over eighty, and containing a number of talented young men. Statistics of the last examination show that there were some twelve who stood above 98 (100 being the maximum). Some few were perfect in every department, and a goodly number came within only a fraction of it.

Our class is as remarkable for talent as the present senior class is for the want of it, and I often hear members of the junior laughing—in a pleasant manner, of course—at those of the senior.

The seniors are now speaking in public from the chapel stage. None of their productions have as yet struck me as peculiarly fine. On the whole the declamation of the boys in Columbia is superior to what it is here. It is, I believe, an established fact that Southerners are more remarkable for their oratorical powers than Northerners.

One of the Georgia students, a classmate—Oscar Lewis, from LaGrange—lost his mother a few days ago. He was much affected by her death, remarking that "his only consolation was that she was a Christian"—though he is by no means such himself.

Dr. Maclean left Princeton on Friday on his way to Scotland, his object being to secure some possession in the line of property. His departure produced quite an impression among the students. Numbers went to his house to bid him farewell; and over a hundred accompanied—or rather preceded—him to the depot. As the cars moved off which bore him away, with hats off they gave nine long and loud cheers for the vice-president of Nassau Hall. The bystanders were perfectly amazed.

(*He picks up his flute.*)

Jenny Lind has excited quite an interest among the inhabitants of New York. Tickets are now selling at $20. One gentleman is said to have paid $130 for a family ticket. Very foolish in him, thinks the present speaker.

(*About to begin playing his flute*)

Jenny Lind was offered $200,000 to cross the Atlantic. Being a very benevolent lady she gives everything away, reserving only so much as will defray her expenses. Only wish her charity would find fit subjects for bestowal in No. 17, North College.

(*He puts down the flute, goes to the desk.*)

Although not very flush of money, still we are at present in no want, for our college bills are all settled, furniture for room purchased, society dues squared, books obtained, and a little surplus on hand.

(*He resumes writing.*)

I hope, my dear parents, you will not deem us expensive, for nothing has been purchased which was not needed.

(*He hears noise outside the window, looks up, smiles.*)

A band of "Indians from the Northwest" passed through this place a short time previous and performed for one night. They proved to be a company of students who, having become low in the purse, resorted to this means to furnish themselves with the desired article.

Last evening a lecture was delivered by a sailor on the question whether whipping and the allowance of liquor should be dispensed with in the navy. Brother went to hear him, and says he gave a horrible account of chastisements inflicted, and of the injurious effects of intoxication. In the progress of his speech a cat-o'-nine-tails was exhibited, with which he demonstrated by repeatedly striking the table. Some say that this person was expelled the navy because of intemperance; others say that, being detected in a theft, and consequently chastised himself, he ran away, and is now going about the country denouncing this custom. To tell the truth, I am verily persuaded that his object is the procuring of money for himself, because this morning a subscription list is passing around.

(*He picks up an apple.*)

The other day Mrs. McCulloh sent us over some apples, for which we were much indebted to her, for every little bit helps.

(*He bites heartily into the apple.*)

Our routine in the refectory is only tolerable: beef, Irish potatoes, and bread, and again (by way of variety) bread, Irish potatoes, and beef—accompanied now and then by a dish of stewed tomatoes. Sometimes a stewed fly is found among the extra articles of diet. Sunday is our best day for eating, for then we have a little more; and this is calculated to last us until another week rolls around. . . . The waiters are generally attentive and obliging—most of them sons of Erin fresh from the mother country.

Nearly all of the servants who attend about college are Irish. They are treated just as we do ours at home; and the only difference is that in the one case they are white and in the other black.

A week ago a general celebration of Negro Sons of Temperance was held in this place, comprising four divisions, one from Trenton, two from Philadelphia, and one from Princeton. They marched through the streets, banners flying, drums beating, with all the pomp and circumstance imaginable. Orations were delivered, I understand, by several of the order; and the whole procession, followed by women and children, proceeded a mile or two out of town to indulge themselves in a picnic. It was a strange sight to those of us from the slave states.

(*He picks up a newspaper.*)

Saw in a Southern paper the other day an account of a public meeting in Liberty County. Was pleased thus to see the county taking her stand in respect to the great question agitating the nation. The bill for prohibiting slavery in the District of Columbia has passed the Senate, but will, I hope, be killed in the House.

I suppose you've noticed the action of the legislature of South Carolina; she seems determined to leave the Union.

(*He pokes the stove.*)

The weather is quite cool, and our thick clothes are constant companions. Our stove answers finely—better even than we anticipated. Now the temperature of the room is pretty nearly equalized, and not as it formerly was—a torrid heat in the chimney and freezing behind.

The smallpox is rather on the increase. Eight cases reported this morning. A white man was buried yesterday who died from the effects of this disease. Brother has been vaccinated twice, and I intend following his example tomorrow.

My old complaint, the headache, has returned with renewed strength—though I do not cease on that account from any of my duties.

(*He goes to the desk.*)

Have been also troubled a little with sore eyes, a complaint from which until this time I have been totally free. They are now, however, stronger and let me study by candlelight.... The gasworks are nearly completed, and we hope soon to enjoy the superior light.

During the last few days two phrenologists have been engaged in delivering lectures in this town, as well as in examining the heads of anyone desirous of having the secret workings of his mind unfolded. It is astonishing how many students have been duped. For my part I was prejudiced against these itinerant lecturers from the fact that whenever they spoke, all that openness which should characterize the action of him who relied upon the truth of his cause was nowhere to be found. In some instances they made egregious blunders with regard to the character of the students. It is, in fact, a very accommodating science (if it may be so termed); for if mistaken in one respect they can always find other bumps, the union of which will assist or counteract *ad libitum* the nature and operation of some other.

Dr. Maclean has returned, and is taking us through the intricacies of the *Oedipus Tyrannus* of Sophocles. It is, I find, a well-supported play—as chaste and elegant as any from the ancient Grecian poets, unless it be the *Hippolytus* of Euripides.

I make it a rule every night before retiring to read a chapter in the Greek Testament. Also ten or twelve pages in Cicero's *De Oratore,* which I am perusing independently of the work we are collegiately studying—namely, Tacitus. When Cicero is completed I shall take up Quintilian. I am passionately fond of these old Latin authors. The style is so fine: great majesty of thought and expression. Gives one such a variety in the choice of words.

It is an endless source of pleasure to be able in this manner to converse with the shades of departed greatness, to mark the great conceptions of their minds. It is surprising how much of the present is borrowed from the past. Even in my limited acquaintance with the classics, I am often surprised when I chance upon expressions and thoughts which previously I had deemed the property of some modern writer. It would afford me much pleasure if only I could enjoy more time for reading; but I am so much occupied with lecture-writing and other college duties that reading must in a great measure be laid aside. However, everything in its season, and this is now the season for collegiate pursuits.

(*He goes to the window, looks out.*)

Last Sabbath every twig and span of grass was covered with a perfect film of ice. In the afternoon the weather moderated somewhat, and there came a hailstorm in miniature, for everything was shedding its robe of ice, and down came the frozen drops of water, rattling against the windows and roofs. Many of the boys have experienced pleasure from skating, but as yet terra firma has been to me the safest foothold.

This reminds me of the slippery path we tread. Just imagine a sleepy junior, eyes half open, rushing out of Old North bound for the chapel. As he reaches the stone steps all covered with ice, see his feet how wild they fly! O my countrymen, what a fall was that! A fippenny at least would I have given to have had my coat wadded. (Or rather, not to appear extravagant, I will say three cents.) But no such luck. Down I went, up again, every idea of sleep having disappeared, and rushed to the chapel with no equal mind.

Dr. Maclean has resumed his evening prayer meetings, and I make it a point to attend regularly.... It would amuse you to see Dr. Maclean walking about the campus in his buffalo robe, all muffled up. I verily believe that if it were required, he could hardly sit still two hours.... We have a report that Dr. Maclean is thinking of taking to himself a rib. For the truth of this report I cannot answer.

(*He looks out of the window.*)

Spring is again robing the earth in a garb of green, and all nature seems buoyant with life.... However, there is not very much of nature here; for you are aware that Jersey is rather a lukewarm state, remarkable for nothing.

The smallpox is disappearing, and will probably soon entirely cease.

(*He goes to the desk, opens a book.*)

It is now a very busy time with us, having to stand the quarterly examination. Today we were wound up for three hours and a half in working original propositions in mathematics—the hardest examination I ever witnessed.

(*He examines his right forefinger with a wince of pain.*)

Last Tuesday the forefinger of my right hand was knocked out of joint by a blow from a shinny stick. It was, however, soon restored to its former position and is now much better, although my hand will not bear squeezing.

Numbers of the students are leaving every day to hear the sweet music that falls from the lips of Jenny Lind. Although desirous to behold so distinguished a personage, still so much is to be done that I scarce would feel satisfied to leave my present duties with such an object in view.

Have been much interested in perusing the works of Dean Swift. Have found much to amuse. His style rather quaint in the *Tale of a Tub,* but fine in *Gulliver's Travels*—that is, easy and natural. His sly hints at the political factions of the day are capital. Here and there, however, he is exceptionable, being rather disposed to indecency.

(*He resumes writing.*)

The examination, which has continued all this week, is now completed, and I will do myself the pleasure, my dear parents, of conversing with you for an hour or two. One of the peculiar privileges which man enjoys is that, although far removed from those we love, still every facility is afforded of a speedy and untrammeled intercourse. Ours is no Russian despotism, where even private letters must pass before a suspecting spy of the tyrant, but a free, independent nation, calling no man master save Him who formed "the earth and all that therein is." With what a filial attachment should every American citizen cleave to this "sweet land of liberty"!

Our grades will most probably be out the first of next week. If mathematics were only dispensed with, I would stand as high as any in the class.

Time is indeed with astonishing rapidity pursuing his way. Year after year rolls round, and before many months have elapsed I shall be abroad upon the world, mingling with men whose characters and lives are as various as the tints of the forest in early autumn.... Of late my attention has been called to the subject of law. It appears to me to be the profession in which I could with most probability hope for success, and my design is to bestow most labor upon those branches which tend to prepare me for that vocation.

Am now engaged in writing my speech for the junior stage. Find it hard to select a subject, and, when chosen, to treat it in a manner which will appear pleasing to the audience. Will write most probably upon the sublime. It is a subject which can hardly be stated in the short space of ten minutes, and I will have therefore to touch barely upon the most prominent points.

(*He leaves the desk, undresses for bed, first in view of the audience, later behind the screen, now and then looking out from behind the screen as he continues talking.*)

Last Saturday we spent a pleasant evening with the Misses Brearley. One of their nieces was with them—a very good-looking lady, although from her appearance I would rather judge her just out of boarding school and consequently unskilled in the arts of polished life. Beauty is captivating, but there is no object in this world that I dislike more than a lady who, though pretty, has not the common sense to carry on a respectable conversation or to show by her conduct that she has refinement and intelligence.... Next to religion a mother should be possessed of a polished and substantial education—not one of those in the present day deemed by many fashionable; for those if analyzed will in the main be found to consist in a smattering of French, a regular graduation in the line of novel-reading, some music, and only a bare outline of history. No wonder we find such a number of affected little beings— the only excitement to obtain the last novel, the acme of their aspirations to flirt with some poor fool who can be duped by their artifices.... Formerly I used to think every lady "almost divine," but now I do candidly believe that they are not one whit behind young men of equal age in every sort of impropriety. Nothing— nothing—could induce me to be yoked with one of those, even if she should hold the purse of Fortuna or be a granddaughter of the nabob of Arcot. Give me a regular Southern lady with a warm heart and a true hand; and if she carry a horn of plenty with her, so much the better.

(*He emerges from behind the screen clad in his nightdress, climbs into bed.*)

No attacks as yet from the *night marauders* concerning which we were so carefully warned—although I heard a student say he found himself almost lugged off bed and bedding by them the other night.

(*He yawns, blows out the candle, pulls up the covers, nestles his head on the pillow, speaks drowsily.*)

Rather prefer their room to their company....

FADEOUT

Act Two

The room of CHARLES COLCOCK JONES, JR., *in Nassau Hall, Princeton, 1851–1852.*
As the stage lights come up, CHARLES *is seated at the window, playing his flute.*

It is a most beautiful night. The moon is shedding her silvery rays on all beneath; a delightful breeze is fanning the brows warmed by the heat of an August sun; all nature in silence seeks quiet repose, as if anticipating the calm of a Sabbath evening; and naught interrupts the stillness of the hour save the song of some late rambler or the occasional chirp of the watchful insect.

I have just returned from a pleasant visit to Mr. and Mrs. McCulloh. Found them viewing Jupiter through a telescope. We also obtained a fine sight of the moon. If those noble ancient astronomers, who labored and toiled to investigate the laws of other worlds, had only possessed the means which we enjoy for investigating the same, what would they not with their minds and perseverance have accomplished?

Last evening we beheld one of the most beautiful sights I ever witnessed. Just over our heads a bright halo of light seemed circling the zenith, ever changing yet always forming anew, assuming varied shapes as if to call forth renewed exclamations of admiration; while ever and anon bright coruscations of light were seen glancing along the north, as if the attendants of Aurora, thinking their mistress slept, were toying with a sleeping world, and bright fairies, stealing rays from her radiant car, were sporting with each other in festive joy. It was the aurora borealis—the first I ever witnessed. The cry of "Heads out!" was echoed and reechoed through the campus, and soon the ground was crowded with boys—some just from the arms of Morpheus, others quitting the student's desk to gaze upon the loveliness of nature.

Just before retiring to bed several of my friends mentioned that they were going upon a serenade and requested my presence. The night was lovely: all nature in quiet repose, even the zephyrs forgetting to breathe, while the moon was beaming with an effulgence soft yet beautiful. Delightfully did the strains of music float upon the midnight air—soft, harmonious, well calculated to break the calm slumbers of fair maidens and awaken the poetic emotions of the soul. A beautiful nosegay was thrown from one of the windows.

(*He goes to the desk, writes.*)

You know not the pleasure that I experience, my dear parents, when, laying aside the accustomed routine of college engagements, I bid my pen trace the feelings of my soul, and politely bargain with Uncle Sam for the safe transmission of a few words of love to those whom my bosom ever holds most dear.... A continued repetition of "the same old news" tires the receiver. I will therefore endeavor to interest you, for a few moments at least, with such reflections as forced themselves upon my mind this evening while taking a short stroll.

I love to walk alone. Not that company is disagreeable; far from it: an interchange of sentiment is pleasant. But there are seasons when one should leave the busy throng, view nature in her silent operations, and above all commune with nature's God.

The sunset this eve was beautiful. Just before the King of Day hasted to plunge beneath those western waters, he seemed loath to leave so lovely a world to the sway of darkness, and turning his full-orbed face full against the horizon, shed his farewell rays, mantling this azure vault with gorgeous drapery, as if to say: "Good night, loved spot of God's creation. Ere I leave thee, take this beauteous covering and wear it in remembrance of me."

But hark! Is that the neighing of some war horse snuffing the battle from afar? 'Tis something yet more terrible, for yonder appears some huge iron monster, whose tread is like the sound of a mighty earthquake. In his nostrils dwell fire and smoke. His mission is onward, his trust three hundred souls. . . . Then, just by his side, a fit companion came—the steamboat puffing along the canal. . . . And on its very brink stand the posts of the telegraphic wires. Yes, the telegraph, that great annihilator of time. Send a dispatch from New York at ten o'clock, and they will receive it in St. Louis a quarter before that hour. Is it not then truly an annihilator of time?

Truly we live in an age of wonders. Could the ancient Roman have arisen from his sleep of ages and stood where I then did, how completely would he have been lost in amazement! Surely he would have imagined that Jupiter and Neptune were running a race; but I fear that his most vivid conceptions regarding the swiftness of a Mercury would have fallen far short of the rapidity of the telegraph.

Have you seen a notice of a recent invention in Washington, by means of which it is proposed to propel locomotives by means of galvanic batteries, thus dispensing with coal, wood, fire, and water? What a triumph of mind over matter!

(*He coughs, resumes writing.*)

Am sorry to say that my old friend the sore throat has again paid me a visit, and seems demanding penance for the long vacation that has been allowed. Have this morning taken a dose of blue pill and salts, with a gargle of alum. . . . The sweet notes of Jenny Lind's voice are still sounding in my ear. Charming lady, may you never catch the sore throat!

We have now fairly entered upon the duties of another college term. . . . An unusually large number of students have arrived this week. Sixty have already been examined and admitted. Among this number there are four native regular Georgians. I soon got on the right side of the young men, stated the case as it stood, and before two hours had elapsed had persuaded them all to enter the Cliosophic Society. Judge Berrien's son also will be introduced, so that we will have five from Georgia entering our hall at the same time. Very good for the Empire State of the South.... We have established a Georgia table in the refectory, and enjoy a sociable meal among ourselves, served à la mode Jersey but eaten Georgia fashion, spiced with Georgia interchange of feeling.

We have been very active in our endeavors after new members for the hall, and we hope to have about two-thirds of the "greenuns." (College term: excuse it, but it is very significant.) It would amuse you to see how very green some of them are: now trying to employ the high-flown language of a metaphor, again perpetrating some miserable pun or piece of worn-out wit; now strutting through the campus as pompously as the nabob of Arcot, with standers so stiff

(*He adjusts his own standers before a mirror.*)

that to encounter a point would be almost to endanger a jugular vein, again trying to use college phrases and almost invariably applying them inappropriately.

In regard to my change of location, I have determined to remain in college. And as they have raised the board in the refectory to $2.50 per week, we are looking forward to better board.

(*He resumes writing.*)

Even so, my dear mother, we shall keep an anxious lookout for the box of good things, as the fare in the refectory is by no means the best in the country.

(*He picks up a peach.*)

We indulged ourselves today by way of variety in a basket of peaches. They were very juicy, but picked too soon and consequently not very sweet. There is a great tendency here to a looseness of the bowels; in fact, there have been scarcely two days in which I have not been more or less affected.

Barnum's Museum was in Princeton on Saturday exhibiting their "wonderful curiosities"—namely, Tom Thumb, the man without arms, elephants with their Asiatic drivers. Above all these, however, Barnum seemed to have imagined that his "car of Juggernaut" would excite most admiration, for it was introduced with great pomp, drawn by eight horses. I expected to find a moving temple, with hideous images of heathen deities, horrid countenances, unearthly forms. At least I thought it would bear some shadow of resemblance to its great prototype, the object of supreme veneration of the Hindu. But instead it consists merely in a large square box on wheels, with a few elephants painted upon its sides.

Well, this immense affair, in view of their not being able to deposit it in any enclosure, was left in the street just in front of Dr. Maclean's house. About twelve midnight seventy or eighty of the boys went to it and examined whether any person was sleeping within or not. Seeing that all was quiet, and the townfolks slumbering in their beds, a large party laid hold of it, rolled it out of Princeton, down to the canal (a distance of about a mile), and there tumbled it in. An iron steamer ran against it in the night, injuring it seriously.

The drivers (about sixty in number) first discovered that it was missing about four in the morning, when they were preparing to take up the line of march for Brunswick. Provoked at seeing their boasted "Juggernaut" missing, they tracked it to the canal; and you may well imagine their chagrin when they found it there, filled with water, covered with slimy mud, and tilted by the steamer into the shape of a rhombus. They made many threats—but not in the hearing of the students. "If we only could catch those chaps," said they, "we would tie them up and cast them one by one into the canal." One declared that he single-handed could whip any twenty students. Having with much difficulty drawn the famous car from its watery grave, they proceeded to mend it up, and by the application of oil or turpentine to remove the dirty deposit upon its sides and top.

Having completed this renovating process, they proceeded to Princeton. Many of the boys were down while they performed this job, and excited them by jocose remarks concerning the dignity of this sacred curricle. Several, in spite of the prohibition of the driver, mounted upon the top and joined in the ride. As they entered the town you could hear them crying: "Here comes the holy car of Juggernaut!" "Here comes Barnum's grand humbug!"

So much for this spree. Everyone in town thought it the best frolic the students have ever had.... Barnum is certainly one of the humbugs of the age. He will doubtless avoid Princeton most carefully in after tours.

(*He looks out of the window.*)

We have been subject to a disagreeable change of weather, but are now blessed with the light of a beautiful sun—an atmosphere as pure as that which we are told is wont to settle upon the fair land of Italy, and a sky so blue and cloudless that a Thomson might have tasked his powers to tell its loveliness. The heavens above seem as if gathering new beauties, while the fall of the leaf and the golden tinge upon the grove betoken the changes of the seasons.

Everything is moving on very smoothly.... Dr. Carnahan preached a fine sermon two Sabbaths since on swearing, and Dr. Maclean followed on the next Sabbath in a tirade on dueling.

Have been for some time attending a sick young man from Georgia—Oscar Lewis, from LaGrange. For the last eight days he has been drunk, having during that time taken some four hundred drinks, or about fifty quarts. You may well imagine his condition. The first night that I sat up with him, he would spring from the bed, roll and toss, and call upon us for "just one more drink." It was certainly one of the most awful sights I have ever seen.

We have had a death recently among our number. Mr. William H. Timlow, a member of our class, died at the residence of his parents in Orange County, New York. He was a devotedly pious young man, beloved by all, diligent in his studies, unpretending in all his duties. The disease which terminated his mortal career was dropsy. Before leaving college he looked very badly; and as I bade him farewell the thought was impressed upon my mind that I should nevermore behold him alive. We are about to make an effort to erect a monument over him. His brother, who is also a member of our class, remarked that such a token of our respect for the dead would be very gratifying to his parents and relatives.

Several students are on the point of being dismissed for gambling, drunkenness, and firing torpedoes in recitation room. They will probably be graduated before their time this evening.

Having just completed our first quarterly examination, I feel more at leisure.... Dr. Torrey has been absent from Princeton during the past week, and we have had no examination with him, and now flatter ourselves that we will escape his sarcastic queries. He has very little respect for a student's knowledge, possesses a fine command of ready wit, and generally expends it upon the heads of those on trial.

The faculty here are a very gentlemanly set, and in by far the majority of cases it is a student's own fault if he does not improve. Just abstract Professor Alexander and let him wander alone amid his labyrinths of hyperbolas and asymptotes and returning curves and cycloids. I will stand with anyone in the other branches; but when he enters in, the heart goes faint, the memory sinks into oblivion, and the whole man shivers, as one shrinking from a grapple with "airy nothing"—or rather "the little end of nothing whittled to a point having neither length nor breadth but merely position."

Last evening our division of speakers was invited over by Dr. Maclean to partake of a supper. The old doctor's fine engravings and book of Shakespeare illustrated were exposed, spiced with anecdotes of a recent visit to Scotland; and you may depend, the chicken salad and ice creams and cakes were not lost upon refec boys used to "light bread and beef." Dr. Maclean reminds me more of one of our regular hospitable Southern gentlemen than almost any other person I have met.

Never have I seen a more perfect model of a kind, benevolent, and tenderhearted professor. Is anyone sick or in distress? Is anyone depressed in spirits? Is anyone poor or deserving of sympathy? Dr. Maclean is ever ready to relieve his every necessity and administer that healing balm of consolation which only the troubled can best appreciate, which none save the kindhearted know how to bestow. Long will I cherish his numerous good deeds, and ever hold his character in lively remembrance.... It is truly astonishing what an influence a professor may deservedly obtain over the minds of students placed under his care. Yet how frequently do we find persons occupying such positions reserved, abstract, phlegmatic, cold.

(*He goes to the desk, writes.*)

We have completed our first quarterly examination, my dear parents, and you will doubtless receive the circulars in a few days.... You will there see that upon two branches—natural philosophy and Locke—I have taken first with a few others.

(*He clears his throat, hesitates.*)

Now for the chemical grade. It appears very small. Yet let me say that by far the majority are smaller than that. Again Dr. Torrey did not call upon me to recite during the entire session, although every lesson was regularly prepared. The only recitation was that for examination. Then he took me not upon the textbook but upon some incidental remarks made in the beginning of the quarter. So you see, that is not the fairest possible estimate of one's proficiency.... His grades are in general very uncertain. He seems to put down just the first number that enters his head. One great cause of this probably is that he cares rather little about the whole matter, is not acquainted with the students, has never given an opportunity to many of them to recite, and is engaged perchance in other occupations which are to him more attractive. In proof of this, the man who passed the best examination in the class, who had recited beautifully, received for a grade 70. Another of a similar stamp, who had made equal progress, 81. Others again, totally ignorant, were presented with 84 and 85; while others still, who had neither recited in class nor at examination, were graded as high as 90. These are facts. Yet far be it from me to attempt anything unfavorable to Dr. Torrey's abilities, or question his motives. He certainly is a beautiful lecturer. We receive no more lectures from him until next session, as he has engagements in New York during the winter.

The day of Thanksgiving was duly regarded in this village, the stores being shut, the churches open, and—by no means the least cause of rejoicing to many—a turkey prepared in the refectory.

(*He looks out of the window.*)

We have been very quiet, with the exception of several petty little sprees—probably the concoctions of minds large enough to fill the breasts of fresh and sophs aspiring after immortality in that line. A few nights since, such honorable gentlemen displayed immense courage and extraordinary daring by setting on fire the entry windows of East and West Colleges. I wish such worthless fellows could all of them be sent off to Botany Bay and there be made to heat fire engines and burn tar kilns.... It is strange indeed how many boys, the moment they enter within college walls, take entire leave of their senses, virtually renouncing all pretensions to decency, propriety, and everything else that pertains to law and order. Boys are here sent to college so young that instead of being absent from home they should be just where Solomon's prime law might be soundly administered at least twice a day. One good paddling would do Judge Berrien's little son, now in the sophomore class, more good than all the studying nominally performed in a week.

However, let us change the subject and speak of matters at once more interesting and pleasing.

(*He returns to the desk, resumes writing.*)

Your valued letters, my dear parents, have been duly received, and it is with no ordinary pleasure that I peruse lines penned by your hands amid the familiar scenes of Georgia.... While you are thus in the midst of such delights, enjoying the mildness and uniformity characteristic of the Southern winter, imagine us in Princeton with a sheet of snow covering everything, while the loud bleak blasts of Boreas, mingled with sleet, are howling around the stern walls of Old North.

(*He leaves the desk, pokes the stove.*)

Yet to the student snugly housed such weather is delightful. I know of nothing that pleases me better than to sit by a fine fire a stormy night, with everything quiet—with no returning tippler hammering at the door, or loafer crying from the entry "Hello, Charlie!"—and there devote myself to study or reading.

I have just finished *The Life of William Wirt,* by Kennedy, in two volumes. Every young man who anticipates engaging in the study of law should read it carefully. His letters to Mr. Gilmer, who was under his care, clearly point out to the young lawyer the only sure way whereby he may merit distinction and pursue his profession with success. Wirt certainly held the pen of a gifted writer. His letters are model performances, evincing an extended knowledge of classical literature and a familiar acquaintance with standard authors. Although not sufficiently guarded in his morals when a young man, still after his second marriage he became a devoted husband, one of the most loving fathers, and, as he himself hopes, a pious man. The fact of his being a poor boy and an orphan at an early age, together with the knowledge that severe application and merit alone raised him to that high and responsible station the duties of which he so long discharged—and that with such honor to himself and country—invests his every triumph with a charm. Effort—renewed effort—forms the burden of every hour. In one of his letters we find this sentiment:

(*He reads.*)

"I have formed in my own imagination a model of professional greatness which I am far—very far—below, but to which I shall never cease to aspire. It is to this model that I compare myself whenever the world applauds, and the comparison humbles me to the dust. But I will not despair, since it is only by aiming at perfection that a man can attain his highest point."

Again we behold him in his letters to his children conveying advice in a beautiful manner. In writing to his daughter he speaks thus:

(*He reads.*)

"The way to make yourself pleasing to others is to show that you care for them. The whole world is like the miller of Mansfield, 'who cared for nobody—no, not he—because nobody cared for him.' And the world will serve you so, if you give them the same cause. Let everyone, therefore, see that you care for them by showing them what Sterne so happily calls 'the small sweet courtesies of life'—those courtesies in which there is no parade, and which manifest themselves by tender and affectionate looks, and little kind acts of attention, giving others the preference in every little enjoyment at the table, in the field, walking, sitting, or standing."

In such private views we trace the quiet, unostentatious communings of his mind; but it is in some intricate case such as the trial of Aaron Burr, where vigorous mental exertion and profound sagacity are required, that we must admire William Wirt as the attorney general of the United States. Never an office-seeker, he had always at his command high appointments, tendered by Presidents Monroe and Jefferson and others high in authority. Did you know that the presidency of the Virginia University was offered him by President Jefferson?

The questions, What shall I do in this world? What station shall I occupy? What good perform? What benefit be to the human race? are of vast importance to a young man just entering upon life, and involve in their answers decisions second alone to that great first question, Whom will ye serve, God or Mammon? Lately the choice of a profession has been constantly before my eyes, and every time there comes along with it that empty void, that rudderless feeling, that conscious want of some great touchstone for the trial of motives and actions, devoid of which man is but at best the creature of fancy, change, caprice, and sin. The great difficulty with most young men seems to be this: they hope to do great deeds, hold important trusts, become the chief of the land; and yet they seem unwilling to labor and toil while others sleep, imagining that favors will spring up as if by some magic wand.

(*He picks up a letter.*)

Received a letter from Sister yesterday. An invitation was therein couched for me to attend a party soon to be given at Miss Gill's school. If I reach Philadelphia in season I will probably accept, as I wish to see some pretty young ladies—at least now and then.

Otherwise one must necessarily remain devoid of the finer polish; for it is the mild, attractive influence of woman that renders the man the gentleman.

Last Saturday we spent a pleasant evening with the Misses Brearley. Enjoyed the privilege of conversing with several real Southern girls—or rather, *in propria lingua,* young ladies. I expect to call upon a fair one tomorrow evening: Miss Lizzie Trigg, from our sister state Tennessee. It really does the soul of man good to meet one from the sunny South in this land of snow and ice and frozen hearts. Go to a warm clime if you would find open hands and lively affections.

(*He looks out of the window.*)

It really does seem that the icy chain of winter is more binding than ever. Last week the ground was covered with snow. Scarcely had this begun to disappear when a new supply descended on Friday, and last night there was an additional fall of several inches. The romance of snowstorms has long since died away with me, for while I admire its purity and beauty, my thoughts are apt to picture the after days when in its stead shall be found naught but a quagmire.

(*He goes to the cabinet, removes a cake, places it on the table.*)

The box—the promised box—with every nicety which man can wish has been received, and I can assure you that its merits have been candidly discussed by dozens of admiring epicures. The oranges were pronounced by many to be the sweetest they had ever tasted; while the cake remains as yet untouched—but how long none can tell.

(*He eyes the cake appreciatively, picks up a knife as if to cut it.*)

Such considerations are in these regions of vast importance, where "light bread and beef" are "all the go." I fear, however, that I do injustice to our culinary department, for once within the memory of man we enjoyed the inexpressible pleasure of pulling at the tough sinews of a regular old *gander,* who, no longer able to afford a tolerable crop of feathers or pay for his meals, was beheaded to gratify the epicurean tastes of refec boys.

(*He puts down the knife.*)

Long may the memory of Washington be cherished! And would that he had been born twice a year, since his birthday brings with it such pleasing recollections!

(*He goes to the desk, writes.*)

Many have lately been sick in college from diarrhea—caused most probably by the bad water. We have had only one pump that will yield any water at all. Water has been brought from the canal for the use of those in town. Refreshing showers have, however, recently descended, relieving the wants of man and beast. While I now write, the cheerful patter of the raindrop may be heard— sweet to the ear in the silence of evening, suggestive of thought and meditation, congenial to study.

Father, I am sorry that I will have to ask you for more funds. Those given me in Philadelphia were not sufficient. Here you will see an account of the manner in which they were expended.

(*He reads.*)

To board at Joline's, before session term, two days	$ 1.12½
To a bedstead	3.00
To a notebook	.87½
Paid into the college treasury	104.00
To subscription to *The Nassau Monthly*	2.00
To subscription to erecting a monument to William H. Timlow, a deceased classmate	4.00
Paid regular dues to Clio Hall	2.75
To a copy of Locke's *Essays*	2.00
Total	119.75

(*He resumes writing.*)

The board has this session been raised considerably, and they make the seniors pay several dollars more for the purchase of chemicals. I now owe $6 for instruction in Italian, $2 for a chemistry, and will have to get one or two more lecture books. I also owe Dr. Schanck something for curing my sore throat. I regret, Father, that I have to ask for more money, but you will see that the expenses incurred were necessary. I expect that $150 will be sufficient.

(*He turns to the audience, laughs.*)

Saw Dr. and Mrs. Hope on last Friday evening. The professor is still as eager after big words and fancy metaphors as a long crane is after the small fry—with this difference, however, that the acquisitions of the crane are more easily managed than those of the professor.

(*He resumes writing.*)

Judge of my pleasure and delight, my dear mother, when I this morning traced upon the back of a letter the impress of your own beautiful hand! Around me are lying differential and integral calculus, astronomy, ancient Roman and Greek authors—all calling upon me to turn and peruse, pointing with warning fingers to the final examination. Yet I must, my dear parents, throw them aside and engage in a far more delightful enjoyment—that of transmitting to you a few items of news.

You must indeed be enjoying yourself in Liberty County. The most delightful season of the year has now appeared, when all nature in her youthful garb invites her admirers to walk forth and admire her beauties.

(*He goes to the window, looks out.*)

Speaking of the charming Southern climate, you can imagine our condition here by picturing to yourself a country overspread by a sheet of dissolving snow, a soil as soft and muddy as the uncertain banks of the river Styx, with not one verdant leaf as yet visible to gladden the eye or harbinger returning spring.

(*He returns to the desk.*)

We seniors are, however, so busily employed in preparing for our final examination that changes of weather pass unnoticed.... This examination will be quite severe, for you know it includes all our studies for four years, and consequently embraces some which I had not an opportunity of attending to in proper season, being away the fresh and soph years.

This period of graduation forms a solemn era in the life of a young man. Hitherto his path has been clearly defined, his plans all matured by wise and prudent friends. Now, however, his apprenticeship is ended, and he feels he has new responsibilities to meet.

As far as I know myself, I wish to be of some use in the world.... My highest hope is that I may one of these days be able to give you, my parents, some substantial assurance that your many labors and cares, as well as your boundless kindnesses, have not been bestowed in vain. My mind is, you know, turned to the law as a profession. Could I become a minister I would esteem it the most exalted and noble office on earth. Yet in law a boundless field lies open for usefulness and honor to him who uses his opportunities aright.

It was with great pleasure that I read your mention, Mother, of the honorable appointment of Uncle Henry as a delegate to the Baltimore Convention. The choice could not have been wiser, and I hope that he will show himself a firm defender of the Democratic faith.... Quite a difference of opinion prevails here with respect to the nomination for President. Many think that the delegates will play the Polk game over again and bring forward some person who is at present little thought of. Mr. Buchanan is my choice, and Mr. Douglas next. Whoever the successful nominee may be, I hope at all events that we will be able to elect him—and that triumphantly. The Democratic flag which has so often floated in victory must not now be suffered to droop in defeat.

Our final senior examination terminated today. All college obligations have now ceased, and we are really graduates, although the degrees will not be officially conferred until the 25th of June.

The examining committee, appointed from the board of trustees, expressed themselves highly pleased—and deservedly so, I am persuaded. The actual fact of the matter is, the members of our class are nearly all of them fine students, and grade high. Over twenty of them have an average throughout the entire course of over 96, and some seven or eight of these range between 99 and 100.

I expect to remain in Princeton until the commencement is

over, as a fine opportunity will be afforded for reading and preparing my speech for the senior stage.

American history and the lives of the great and good of this our favored land possess countless charms for me; and I have accordingly commenced the perusal of the biographies of the most prominent characters who have assisted in rearing this mighty republic. The heroes we worship were men actuated by no love of kingly honors. They came forth as the people's representatives, pure in heart, with singleness of aim, relying upon the justice of their cause.

Few appreciate aright the comprehensive nature of our Constitution; hence the necessity for such men as may prove not confounders but true expounders of its glorious principles. It is a serious evil that these glorious principles have of late been so much prostituted to suit the ends of designing men, and support the pretensions of those whose aims are really in direct opposition to its spirit.

Consider the orators of the American Revolution. Seldom do we find at any one period such an array of talent, such intrepid action, such precious models for the imitation of the young. What an example of stern true patriotism and devotion to the calls of country does the life of Patrick Henry exhibit! With a generous devotion that knew no fear, with a voice tremulous with patriotic rage, with an eye flashing unutterable fire, he exclaimed: "Give me liberty, or give me death!"

(*He picks up a book.*)

Lord Chatham in a speech delivered in the House of Lords thus speaks of our great men:

(*He reads.*)

"When you consider their decency, firmness, and wisdom, you cannot but respect their cause and wish to make it your own. For myself, I must avow that in all my reading—and it has been my favorite pursuit—for solidity of reasoning, force of sagacity, and wisdom of conclusion, no nation or body of men can stand in preference to the general congress at Philadelphia."

If this be the opinion of the distinguished English statesman, how should we study their illustrious lives and emulate their example! Would that at the present time more of this spirit of '76 could be seen in the actions of individuals—both public and private!

When we recur to those scenes which tried the souls of our ancestors; when we read the burning eloquence of an Otis, or dwell with rapture upon the inspiration of a Henry; above all when we rest our eye upon the Father of his Country, majestic in person, in thought, in daring—then does the bosom swell with the proudest emotions, and we exclaim with our honored statesman: "This—this is eloquence, or rather it is something more than all eloquence; it is action—noble, sublime, godlike action."

My subject for the senior stage is "Action in America." They tell me that I was one of the prominent candidates for the valedictory; yet this honor was awarded to Dr. Magie's son because of his higher grades and longer connection with the institution. There are several in the class who, I am persuaded, can do much better than he; yet let me in no manner detract from his honors.

On last Sabbath Dr. Carnahan delivered his farewell sermon to the graduating class. His remarks were most touching; and his kind advice and fatherly counsel came with melting power from those venerable lips. Truly he is a great and good old gentleman. I feel much attached to the majority of the members of the faculty, and to many of the students; and the heart grows sad when it reflects that all these associations and friendships are so soon to be dissolved.

(*He looks out of the window.*)

Our campus now looks beautifully. Summer has completely usurped the throne of spring, and the trees are already robed in their richest green. Today several mowers are in the campus, cutting the grass, which is now some two feet in length. They are making many preparations for the approaching commencement, and we will look as fine as a fiddle by that time. From all accounts such anniversaries are well attended. Ladies flock to Princeton from New York, Philadelphia, Trenton, and all the country around.

(*He goes to the desk, writes.*)

I write, my dear parents, to convey a pressing invitation from Mrs. McCulloh that you will remain with them during commencement. They say that the hotel at that season is so much crowded with country people, and frequented by drinking characters, that it would not only be very unpleasant but almost impossible to put up there. You will, if you accept, spend a delightful period with them, for they are truly Southern in their hospitality and feeling. No refusal will be taken, for she requested me to bring you there immediately upon your arrival, and says that she will expect you on Monday.

It only remains, Father, for me to request that you would send me ten dollars. The senior orators have to get out bills of the proceedings of the night when they speak, and also assist in defraying the expenses for music then incurred.

Professor Hope in one of his lectures advised us never to write when we had nothing to say, and always to stop when we had finished; so as I am bound to pay due deference to the instructions of those having authority, I shall close. Hoping, my dear parents, to see you next week, I remain, with warmest love to you both, and howdy for all the servants, your affectionate and devoted son, Charles C. Jones, Jr., A.B.

FADEOUT

Voices of Pride

Voices of Pride is drawn exclusively from the letters of Charles Colcock Jones (1804–1863), Mary Jones (1808–1869), Charles Colcock Jones, Jr. (1831–1893), and Mary Sharpe Jones (1835–1889), written from 1854 to 1860, and now preserved in the libraries of the University of Georgia (Athens) and Tulane University (New Orleans).

FATHER (The Rev. Dr. Charles Colcock Jones), *a gentleman in middle life*

MOTHER (Mrs. Mary Jones), *a lady in middle life*

SON (Charles Colcock Jones, Jr.), *an attractive, intelligent young man in his twenties*

DAUGHTER (Mary Sharpe Jones), *an attractive, intelligent young woman in her twenties*

The scene is set in Cambridge, Massachusetts, and coastal Georgia (Savannah and nearby Liberty County) from 1854 to 1860.

NOTE

The DAUGHTER does not participate in the main action of the play, but provides something of a subplot; she also serves as something of a chorus, marking the transition from scene to scene. She stands apart from the other three characters, always speaking directly to the audience, taking them into her confidence.

Act One

As the stage lights come up, the FATHER *is pacing about, dictating a letter. The* MOTHER *is seated at a desk, acting as amanuensis, responding to the dictated text from time to time with gestures and facial expressions communicating agreement and strong support.*

FATHER: Sir, you entered my family on a friendly arrangement for copying my church history, on your own proposal, the 28th of July a year ago, and left it on the 20th of September following. You were introduced to me as an educated man, the son of a highly esteemed minister of South Carolina, whose full name you bear; as a married man, having but recently married your second wife, who was then absent at the North for her health; as a prominent member of the Presbyterian church in Columbus, Georgia, the superintendent of the Sunday school, the president of the Young Men's Christian Association, and the principal of a female high school in that city, and recommended on your school circular by names of the first respectability. You had also taught a school within the bounds of our own congregation here in Liberty County, and had associated with the active members of the church resident in the village, and I believe had aided them in their efforts to give religious instruction to the Negroes. You came to my acquaintance under these favorable circumstances, and were received for what you professed yourself to be—a gentleman, a married man, and a Christian. You rendered yourself agreeable, and conducted yourself with every mark of respect and propriety; you were always present morning and evening at family worship, and sometimes took part in that worship. You were the guest of a gentleman, a professing Christian and a minister of the gospel; and you witnessed from week to week his efforts to instruct religiously the servants of his family and household.

(*He checks with a glance to be sure that the* MOTHER *is keeping up with his dictation.*)

You were under my roof but a short time before you debauched a young Negro girl—a seamstress, and one of our chambermaids. And you continued your base connections with this Negro woman week after week until you took your final leave! Of the hundreds of men of all classes and conditions and professions—men of the church and men of the world, married and unmarried—who have been guests in my house for days, weeks, months, and some for years, you, William Henry Burdoch, are the only man who has ever dared to offer to me personally and to my family and to my neighbors so vile and so infamous an insult. You are the only man who has ever dared to debauch my family servants, and to defile my dwelling with your adulterous and obscene pollutions. Had you been detected, I should have driven you instantly out of the house and off the premises with all the accompanying disgrace which you merited; and I regret that the law affords me no redress under so serious an indignity and injury.

(*He checks again to be sure that the* MOTHER *is keeping up with his dictation.*)

The proof of your criminality is of so clear a character as to remove all doubt. There is the free, unconstrained confession of the Negro woman herself in full detail. There is the correspondence between the time of your connection with her and the birth of the child—a mulatto, now some time born. And there is a resemblance to you beyond mistake. In this last proof I do not rely upon my own convictions. I have submitted the child to the inspection of three gentlemen in the county who know you well personally and are acquainted with your physiognomy, and they without hesitation declare its resemblance to you to be as striking as possible. And all who have seen it are of the same opinion. The evidence is amply sufficient to warrant the submission of the case to the session of the Columbus church for action.

And now, sir, what are your former Christian friends to think of you? You have sinned under the most forbidding and aggravating circumstances, and it is difficult to conceive of a more degrading and hypocritical course of wickedness and folly, or one which argues a greater destitution of principle or more callousness of conscience. I never have been more deceived in a man in all my life. How have you brought disgrace upon religion! What an injury have you done to the soul of the poor Negro! What disgrace and ruin of character have you brought on yourself! I pity you, and try to pray for your redemption. . . . I voluntarily offered you my name on your school circular. I request you to take it off. You have betrayed my confidence and injured me grievously, and I cannot look upon you as I once did, nor hold any further intercourse with you.

(*He goes to the desk, takes up the pen, and signs the letter.*)

MOTHER: I think you have said all that is necessary to be said, and in a faithful and Christian manner. There is nothing written which you need ever desire should be blotted out.

FATHER (*commencing to dictate another letter*): My dear son. . . .

(*The* MOTHER *takes up the pen. During the course of this letter the* MOTHER *and* FATHER *reveal to the audience, through appropriate gestures and facial expressions, their intense sympathy and close affection for each other.*)

I do not think that anyone wrote you last week. I did not, it having been a busy week. Mother is always busy, you know, and has had company. . . . She rises about six in the morning, or now half-past five; takes her bath, reads, and is ready for family worship about seven; then breakfasts with a moderate appetite and enjoys a cup of good tea. Breakfast concluded and the cups washed up and dinner ordered, Little Jack gathers up his "weepons," as he calls them, and follows his mistress, with her sunbonnet on and her large India-rubber-cloth working gloves, into the flower and vegetable gardens. Here she spends sometimes near two hours hoeing, planting, and pruning, Little Jack and frequently Beck and several other little fellows and Gilbert in the bargain all kept as busy as bees about her—one sweeping, another watering, another weeding, another planting and trimming, and another carrying off the limbs and trash.

About ten her outdoor exercise is over, and she comes in, sets aside her bonnet, draws off her gloves, and refreshes herself with a basin of cool water, after which she looks that the house has been put in perfect order. She now devotes herself to cutting out, planning, fitting, or sewing, giving attention to the clothing department and to the condition of furniture, curtains, towels, and linens.

Meanwhile the yards have been swept, the walk sanded, and Patience has her culinary world all in neat order. The fowls have scattered themselves everywhere in the lot, crowing and cackling and scratching; the sheep have finished their early browse, and are lying down beneath the great hickory tree; and overhead and all around is one general concert of birds.... The glorious sunlight, the soft south wind, and the green earth and the blue heavens— Mother sees and enjoys it all; but she is too busy now to come out and take a view. If she has visitors, she is sitting at work and in conversation with them, or for an hour or two before dinner takes her book or pen in hand. Sometimes she indulges in a quiet little doze, and gets up refreshed just before we are called to dinner.

For an hour or two after dinner she retires, and about the middle of the afternoon makes her appearance dressed for the evening. Then she is full of her uniform cheerfulness, and attracts everybody to her—husband, children, servants, visitors, old and young.... The sea breeze is blowing sweetly. Our friends have driven over; the horses have been taken from the carriage, and the drivers have gone to pay their calls in the servants' quarters. The chairs are set out in the piazza, and here we spend a social hour and take tea. Our friends take leave, and then we have family worship. Sometimes they unite with us before they go. We all retire now to our rooms, and when the business of the day is over, then Mother enjoys the quiet, and loves to sit up reading and writing and conversing. She says this is the pleasantest part of the *day* to her.

(*The* MOTHER *looks up at the* FATHER *in amusement.*)

SON: Your very welcome letter, my dear father, presenting me in such charming colors with all the pleasures which you are now enjoying at home, and especially with the engagements and recreations of dear Mother, was yesterday morning received. To me the picture, always so attractive, is rendered even more dear in consideration of the bloody scenes which are now hourly transpiring in our very midst.... Here in Boston mob law, perjury, free-soilism, and abolitionism are running riot. For two days I have been in the courthouse attending this trial. The room is filled with armed men; even the counsel at bar have their revolvers and bowie knives.... I will not enter upon any account of the proceedings. These you will find contained in the papers, which I will send you daily. It is yet quite doubtful whether the Negro Burns will be sent back or not. Six witnesses have been introduced today in the defense, who testify that they saw Burns in Boston *more than three weeks* before ever he left Virginia. *Flat perjury.* My blood boiled at this Negro testimony, at the vile epithets heaped up upon Colonel Suttle by counsel.

MOTHER: My dear child, I cannot tell you the deep anxiety I feel on your account, exposed as you are to scenes calculated to exasperate your feelings.

SON: Colonel Suttle is a perfect Virginia gentleman, of high standing, well educated, of fine, commanding appearance. For two days I have sat at his side, conversed with him freely in and out of court, and consequently entertain for him not only such sentiments of regard as a high-minded, generous person should receive from anyone, but also such an attachment as only a Southerner can know for his brother Southerner when he finds him in a land of abolitionists, conspiring not only against his property but his *life*.

FATHER: I am glad, my dear son, that you were with Colonel Suttle and gave him sympathy and support.

MOTHER: Although he appears to be a gentleman capable of any emergency, yet as a gentleman he would and no doubt did appreciate your attentions and those of the other young gentlemen from the law school.

SON: That Colonel Suttle is the legal owner of Burns is denied by no one. His claim is perfect; naught but flat palpable perjury instigated by abolitionism can hold the contrary for an instant.

FATHER: I agree with you that the conduct of the abolitionists is infamous. They demonstrate themselves in this case to be fanatics of the worst sort, setting at defiance all laws human and divine, the constitution of their country, all truth, all decency, without one redeeming quality.

MOTHER: Not even the common courage of men!

SON: Do not be surprised if when I return home you find me a *confirmed disunionist.*

MOTHER: I am thankful, my dear son, that you will soon be removed from such an atmosphere of abolitionism and every evil work.

SON: Our professor, Judge Loring, deserves the approbation of the entire country for the manly, open, and determined manner in which he conducted himself during the trial and finally disposed of the case. You have no idea what indignities he endured. Some of the abolition ladies of Boston, I understand, sent him thirty three-cent pieces; and upon the package in which they were enclosed was written: "The price of blood." You will understand at once the blasphemous allusion.

FATHER: Boston is a remarkable city, and seems to be in a fair way of working out fame of some sort.

SON: In our lecture room at Cambridge several of the viler species of abolitionists—members of the law school—so far forgot even such gentlemanly bearing as belonged to them (although I must confess as a general thing very little obtains in the genus *abolitionist*) as to indulge in hissing.

MOTHER: Hissing!

SON: For a second only could the notes of these geese be

distinguished, and then old Dane Hall shook to the very center with the thunders of welcome and shouts of approval to him who had in such trying times sustained the honor of his school, his city, his state, his country.

MOTHER: Your professor came out with flying colors.

SON: I could scarcely refrain from leaving my seat and forcibly ejecting from the room, by a stout application of boot leather, a puny scoundrel who was hissing in one corner of the room. But respect for the school and myself forbade such a course.

FATHER: The creatures of the law school hissed him as he came into the lecture room! They should have been *expelled* by the college authorities.

MOTHER: The Southern and right-minded students did well to *cheer* him.

SON: You have, I hope, received the papers which I forwarded containing a minute account of all the incidents of trial, the excitement in Boston, and the final rendition of the fugitive. The powerful military force on the ground is all that prevented Boston from becoming one miserable arena of riot and blood and lawlessness.

FATHER: I do think the Bostonians deserve credit for the execution of the law. They did execute it; and the whole matter will do good in our country—even in New England itself. The effect over the Union will be adverse to the cause of abolitionism and disunion.

MOTHER: It is a pity the *instigators* of rebellion could not be reached and punished.

SON: It is really surprising to what an extent a person becomes an actual fool who, possessed of one prejudice, one misconceived idea, surrenders himself a total slave to its miserable influence.

FATHER: I do not at all regret that you have been an eye- and ear-witness to all this matter. You will see what human nature is under fanatical influences, what nerve is required of men in facing mob violence, and how necessary is self-possession for the vindication of right.

MOTHER: You will see also the silent, potent majesty of the law.

FATHER: You will learn also the nature of abolitionism in its pure unadulterated infidel form; the New Englanders will drink their fill of it.
MOTHER: And you will see also that there is *power* in our government.
FATHER: Gather experience from all these things; make your observations; and learn self-control under circumstances of excitement and danger.
SON: On last Friday I was highly honored by the assembly of Dane Law School in being elected the first speaker of the senior class for the present session.
MOTHER: We hear with great pleasure, my dear son, of the honor conferred by your election as speaker of the assembly.
FATHER: Your election took us rather on a surprise, you being a Southerner, and there being so much anti-Southern feeling in that region of country.
MOTHER: May it all perish soon!

DAUGHTER: It is now time, as Father would say, that "all honest folks had gone to bed"; but as this is a season when the young ones are permitted to "sit up" a little longer than usual, I suppose I may be excused if I am not found one of the aforesaid class tonight. . . . This morning before six my slumbers were disturbed by Dunwody's "Merry Christmas! Merry Christmas, Cousin Mary! I've caught you!" I really enjoyed seeing his delight, for I well remember the great pleasure I used to feel in being the first to announce this season of festivity. . . . I was so nicely caught this morning that I must really tell you of it. When I met Aunty in Mother's room, she wished me a Merry Christmas, and said she hoped the next would find me married. I replied: "I hope so too!" And much to my confusion Father answered from behind the screen: "You *do,* do you? Tired of the old folks, are you?" "Oh!" said I (for I had nothing else to say), "Father, I really did not know that you were behind the screen!" . . . By the way, while this topic is under consideration, I will just give you a leaf from Dame Report's recent publication,

Facts Relative to Matrimony. Laura Jones's engagement with the Rev. Mr. Bowman is broken off. They *say* because *she* could not be married immediately, *he* would not wait. I do really think that any young minister who breaks engagements ought to be disciplined in some way. And I do not mean to confine this remark to clergymen alone.... I must now bid you good night, for I feel it is time for me to be enjoying myself in another land. So good night!

MOTHER (*opening a letter and reading*): "Reverend and dear sir, on the 30th ultimo William Henry Burdoch of this place showed to the subscribers (members of the session of the Presbyterian church of Columbus) a letter from you addressed to said Burdoch containing a charge against him of a very serious character—namely, adultery—and that, too, under very aggravating circumstances. If the charge be true as stated, we could not be astonished at any degree of indignation and contempt that might be felt and manifested by the injured party."

FATHER (*dictating his reply as the* MOTHER *acts as amanuensis*): I thank you for your kind appreciation of my feelings in so unhappy an affair.

MOTHER (*reading*): "Mr. Burdoch most positively, solemnly, and unequivocally denies the charge altogether. He submitted the letter to us as members of the church session for such action in the matter as might be deemed necessary."

FATHER: I left Mr. Burdoch to act as he chose; and he has done what he could not well have left undone: he has submitted the case himself.

MOTHER (*reading*): "Now, dear sir, the evidence is what the session wants if it takes any action in the matter. And in such cases reliable legal evidence is what is usually most difficult to obtain. You appear to be fully satisfied of the fact. There may be circumstances connected with such cases that may produce conviction in the minds of those well acquainted with them, but it may not be practicable to produce such evidence as would warrant a conviction by an investigating tribunal."

FATHER: This at times is most unfortunately so—unfortunately so for the innocent, as they must ever lie under suspicion; and unfortunately so for the guilty, as they escape punishment.

MOTHER (*reading*): "In looking at the evidence so far as it appears by your letter, it is: first, the birth of a mulatto child at a time corresponding to the time Mr. Burdoch was in your family; second, the declarations of the mother of the child; and, third, the resemblance of the child to the accused.... The first part of the evidence—time—is satisfactory as far as it goes.... The second—the mother's declaration—is what usually has to be mainly relied upon in similar cases when the mother is a free white woman; but courts and juries have not always convicted the accused when the mother's declaration upon oath has been positive. In a majority of cases the mother, being the complainant and a free white person, has pleaded *promise of marriage.* In this case such plea could not be urged, for in addition to the fact of Mr. Burdoch's being a married man, the law of the country does not tolerate such marriages."

FATHER: The plea drawn from the illicit intercourse of whites under promise of marriage is irrelevant, since no contracts obtain between whites and blacks.

MOTHER (*reading*): "It is the opinion of some of our ablest legal men who have had much experience in the investigation of cases of bastardy that the propensity in woman is to conceal the true father. The cases that differ from this, they say, are the exceptions, and usually arise from a spirit of revenge for what the woman considers a breach of promise, false pretenses, etc. Now, dear sir, the fact is apparent that your woman, the mother of the child, can plead no breach of promise of marriage. She gave no alarm of any coercive measures having been used. Her own declaration is the only positive evidence."

FATHER: It is not essential to the truthfulness of the mother's declaration that she was not forced and gave no alarm. The consent of the woman was all that was required, and her declaration is that she so consented, and that she had repeated criminal conversation with the said Burdoch, and that the mulatto child is his. And she makes the declaration without revenge and without compulsion.

MOTHER (*reading*): "The third part of the evidence—to wit, resemblance—is of very doubtful character at best. You can doubtless readily call to mind the very striking resemblance that is often found to exist between persons where there can be no kindred, and then again the absence of resemblance between brothers and sisters, parents and children, where the fidelity of the parents would not be questioned by anyone acquainted with them."

FATHER: These are rare exceptions when you compare man with man, and the members of the same families with each other. And the exceptions prove the rule. The resemblance of progeny to parent is *a law of nature,* and runs through the whole animal kingdom, and can neither be gainsaid nor resisted. The resemblance of the mulatto child to Mr. Burdoch is uncommonly and unmistakably distinct and perfect.

MOTHER (*reading*): "Let us turn aside a moment and look at the parties. The woman is a servant—a slave. We have no doubt but that she has been carefully trained and instructed in morals and religion—that she has been taught to observe the strictest rules of chastity. But all this is true of Mr. Burdoch, and in addition thereto he has a character to sustain for himself and his family; and his success in the vocation in which he is engaged must depend in no small degree upon the purity of character he may sustain."

FATHER: The party of the first part is the woman—a Negro and a servant, whom you doubt not has been well instructed and morally and religiously brought up. But servants are not always liars, and are particularly slow to father their children upon white men without the best of reasons. The careful training of our servant has proved no defense. She says "Mr. Burdoch told her not to make him known if anything should happen." ... The party of the second part is Mr. Burdoch, who you say has also been well and religiously trained, is respectably connected, has a character to sustain, a family to support, his success in business is dependent upon his good reputation. The circumstances of Mr. Burdoch to which you allude as well calculated to bind him to a life of integrity and virtue are forbidding enough against a life of contrary character, and were all fully drawn out in my letter to him. But in themselves they do not prove him innocent of the charge preferred against him by the Negro girl, although backed by his denial. They afford ground of presumption that he would not perpetrate so vile a crime, but nothing more. Previous good character and standing may mitigate the sentence of condemnation or aggravate it, just as those who try a case are led by the testimony to view it, but can never be admitted of the nature of proof against charges of wrongdoing. Otherwise some of the greatest offenders would escape justice.

MOTHER (*reading*): "So far as is known to the subscribers, Mr. Burdoch has always sustained a fair character."

FATHER: So far as was known *to me,* Mr. Burdoch when he came to my house had sustained a fair character. But to my amazement, after he left my house I learned that he had been charged by a Negro girl in the village where he taught school in our county with having had criminal connection with her and with being the father of the child with which she was then pregnant; that he had denied the charge before the trustees of the academy and demanded that the Negro should be punished, which punishment was inflicted previously to the birth of the child; and the trustees acquitted him, there being no evidence but that of the Negro girl against him. The Negro girl, however, persisted under punishment that he was the father of the child. The child was afterwards born, and born a mulatto, and she persists in the charge to this day. Now, here are two Negro women living twenty miles apart, without any knowledge of each other, preferring the same charge against the same man and holding to it.

MOTHER (*reading*): "The character of Mr. Burdoch is in great jeopardy, and with his character go his prospects for success even in his secular vocation."

FATHER: You cannot be more surprised nor grieved than I have been, nor more desirous of seeing Mr. Burdoch cleared—not on technical grounds for want of legal evidence to convict, but upon absolute grounds of innocency, there being no evidence of any kind to convict him. But in my judgment this is impossible.

MOTHER (*reading*): "Suppose the church session should take action in the case upon the facts as presented by your letter and should pronounce Burdoch guilty. What would be said of the action by an appellate court?"

FATHER: If my servant were a white woman, with the evidence before you, she would carry a prosecution for bastardy against him in any common court of justice.

MOTHER (*reading*): "Mr. Burdoch from the first declared his willingness to swear to his innocence. He has now done so, and a copy of his statement of denial of the charges under oath is herewith enclosed."

FATHER: Mr. Burdoch denied from the beginning; his denial under oath makes no change in my own convictions. Acquaintance with persons charged with crimes, both ecclesiastical and civil, has taught me to rely for the truth more upon the evidence than upon the asseverations of the accused.

MOTHER (*reading*): "I, being session clerk, request that from your extensive experience in church judicature you will please suggest what course should be adopted here by the session."

FATHER: It would be highly improper in me to suggest what course should be adopted by your session, as this would carry me beyond my sphere, being neither prosecutor nor member of your session. And also unnecessary, since I have laid pretty fully all the evidence before you.

MOTHER (*reading*): "Will you become prosecutor, or can the session of the church take action?"

FATHER: With the first six chapters of our book of discipline in your hands, you are well able of yourselves, independent of all assistance, to decide what course should be pursued without the intervention of any prosecutor at all.

MOTHER (*reading*): "We do not write to you for the purpose of screening Mr. Burdoch from the full measure of any penalty which he may have incurred; but he is a member of the church of which we are officers; and while we grant that it is our duty to look closely to all offenders, yet it is no less our duty to protect and defend innocent members of the church."

FATHER: I do highly honor the charity and integrity you manifest—charity to protect as far as possible the character of the innocent, and integrity in searching into the matter in order that you may carry out the discipline of the church to the fullest extent necessary without respect of persons, and so preserve the purity and character of Christ's Church, over which He has set you as rulers.

(*He goes to the desk, takes up the pen, and signs the letter.*)

DAUGHTER: At this moment I am serenaded by the screaming of two young owls. You will think, I expect, that we have a strange collection of pets! We have not had the owls quite two days. They are the funniest-looking things you ever saw. . . . What say you to my having two cats and seven kittens? The kittens belong to Duchess, and she is as proud as mothers in general. Don't you want some of the kittens sent on to you by express? . . . And now let me ask you what did you mean by writing me that you had been "so much *engaged,*" underscoring the word in the most special manner? Engaged? When? How? To whom? If you have a secret, please make confession to a friend!

FATHER: My dear son, I wish you to make up your accounts and let me know precisely how much more you will need to settle everything in Cambridge and buy your books and come home, that I may make arrangements; for funds are nearly exhausted, and it will be some time before we can get anything to market.

SON: You wish me, Father, to state precisely how much more money I will need. I have estimated the same, and will state the sum at four hundred dollars.

FATHER: Four hundred dollars. . . .

SON: I hope, Father, that it will not put you to inconvenience to send me this.

MOTHER: Four hundred dollars. . . .

SON: Everything in Cambridge has been steadily advancing in price. Board which at first could be obtained at three dollars per week cannot now be had under five; and rooms which the first session were worth only two dollars or two and a half are now three dollars and over. And everything else—washing, fuel, everything—has proportionably advanced. It seems to be the determination of Cambridge to support itself entirely from gains derived from students.

FATHER: Your expenses have been greater than we anticipated.

MOTHER: I presume you have been economical and put your funds to good use?

FATHER: Have you kept an *account* of your expenses?

SON: I should be sorry, my dear parents, to have you believe that I have been extravagant. Law books can be more reasonably procured here than in Savannah, and there are some forty volumes which it will be necessary for me at the time of leaving Cambridge to have. Law books are, you know, the most expensive of all professional works; the uniform price per volume ranges from three to six dollars. My greatest passion is for books, and somehow or other a bookstore has such an attraction that I am tempted to visit it perhaps rather too often, my purse suffering meanwhile.

MOTHER: In your infancy books were your playthings; at one time you always slept with one.

SON: I am trying to make good use of my time and opportunities, and I hope that the sum here and now invested in the acquisition of my profession will at no distant period yield an interest if not large at least by no means meager.

MOTHER: I feel thankful, my dear son, that we have thus far been able to afford you the best advantages our country provides in obtaining your profession without running in debt.

FATHER: I have requested Mr. Montgomery Cumming of Savannah to forward you a check on Boston for four hundred dollars, the amount you say you will need to get books and clothing and bring you home.

MOTHER: The people, my dear son, are much pleased to hear that you are expected home in a few weeks.

SON: I am happy to learn that they sometimes inquire after me.

FATHER: We are looking forward with fond anticipations to your return, and are counting the weeks.

MOTHER: Be sure and bring your diploma from the law school.

FATHER: In relation to your settlement in life, my dear son, I wish you to exercise your preference and discretion. Do not confine yourself to the South if any other part of the Union is more agreeable to you. And I wish to make the impression upon you with the point of a diamond that you never can attain to eminence in your profession if you have anything at all to do with the management of Negro property.

MOTHER: Planting requires such a consumption of time, and the property you manage makes such a draft upon your attention, that no student and professional man can prosper under it all.

FATHER: I wish you to make up your mind to live by your profession and to be *totus in illis.* Nor shall your patrimony—whatever we have to give you—be in any way endamaged by your having nothing to do with any other pursuit than that of your profession.

MOTHER: This, my very dear son, has been your twenty-third birthday. When I think of you in the past as our own affectionate, dutiful, and upright child, the review is very pleasant. As my mind stretches on to the future, anxiety increases. The period of childhood and youth, of study and preparation, is soon to cease. You are now to come forth as a man amongst men. Your character, your principles, your conduct will indicate your future position in society, your usefulness, and your happiness. Would, my child, that as your mother I had been more faithful to you in example and in precept! The Lord forgive all my neglect and failures in duty!

DAUGHTER: As you may have imagined, Brother Charlie's unexpected arrival surprised us very much. Mother and myself were on our way to the Sand Hills, but we concluded to wait at Montevideo until the stage came, in order that we might get our letters and possibly learn the exact time of his arrival. Judge then our surprise and delight when, as we turned the corner at the Boro, we discovered

Brother Charlie seated upon a trunk!... Brother Charlie begins to feel a little anxious to get to his studies, and talks of going sometime next week to Savannah.... He is now reading aloud downstairs, and I must join the circle, so please excuse me.

SON: After parting with you, my dear parents, and trying to see, as we sailed down the river, whether with the glass I could recognize anyone in the piazza at Montevideo, we had a favorable passage, and reached Savannah the next day at half-past two.... Savannah, as far as I have had an opportunity of judging, appears to be a pleasant city for residence. There seems to be a spirit of comity prevailing among the members of the bar, and there are many lawyers here who will compare favorably with any I have ever seen. Mr. Ward I find a very agreeable gentleman: exceedingly companionable, ready to answer any inquiry, and admirably informed as to the conduct of courts in this state. He advises that I apply for admission to the bar in May at the session of the superior court in this city.

MOTHER: In May....

SON: Between that time and the present I have much to accomplish. My books I unpacked and arranged this evening. My next step is to find more fully what is in them.

FATHER: I have no doubt, my dear son, that if you are patient and apply yourself as I know you can, and adhere by God's assistance to a life of integrity and virtue, you will succeed in your profession.

MOTHER: We would urge upon you a due attention to exercise and diet and regimen. A person of your full habit must have exercise and temperance in all things in order to preserve health.

FATHER: Knowing Savannah well, and the social habits of the people, I do hope you will be careful of the intimacies you form, and depart not from the principles of total abstinence.

MOTHER: I feel assured you will avoid the evening resorts of idle and intemperate men.

FATHER: There is much to be gained in the labor of life by a proper beginning, and upon right principles.

MOTHER: All that is left for your parents now is to commend you constantly to the merciful care of God, and to invoke for you every blessing at His hands.

FATHER: You can never cease to be to them an object of fond solicitude, and we shall ever take the liveliest interest in everything that relates to your welfare.

MOTHER: We hope that you will ever consider us your best friends, and as such freely and fully communicate with us at all times.

SON: The week has passed rapidly away, and my time has been fully occupied. Have nearly finished the Judiciary Act of 1799, and will soon take up the penal code.

FATHER: My dear son, will you call on Mr. William Wright, the real and personal estate broker, and learn from him: Whether he receives and sells Negro property, and on what commissions and expenses.

MOTHER: Whether he buys on his own account.

FATHER: Whether he is able to sell without delay to persons in the up country.

MOTHER: What would be the probable value sold in the up country of a family consisting of father, mother, and five children.

FATHER: Father forty-five, mother forty-six, two girls nineteen and fourteen, and three boys twenty-one, sixteen, and twelve.

MOTHER: All healthy and good-looking; the mother a superior house servant and seamstress.

FATHER: Whether all could be sold to one master without separation.

MOTHER: You know the family we allude to. We feel that there is a limit to patience, and perhaps—*perhaps*—they may do better in other hands.

FATHER: Some, not all of them.

MOTHER: We do not wish to separate them, and let all go together.

FATHER: In conversing with Mr. Wright mention no names, and of course enter into no agreements. Let me have the result of your inquiries.

MOTHER: There may be other and better brokers in town of whom you might also inquire.

FATHER: And another question: Could they be easily sold in Savannah to one man?

MOTHER: And at what probable value?

DAUGHTER: And now what shall I say to interest you? I have drawn a snow scene, and I took it to Savannah to have it framed; and I must tell you it has been much admired. I have another picture loaned me by my drawing teacher there, and I am encouraged to copy it, notwithstanding the formidable appearance of four mules and five pedestrians! I do not think that my talent for animal-drawing is very remarkable.... We saw Mr. Goulding a few evenings ago, and he said that he felt so badly about having gone to sleep in the cars that he came very near writing us a letter of apology. Aunty said she hoped he had waked up. "Oh," he said, "I hope in a short time to wake up to some very pleasant realities!" His marriage will take place on the 18th of this month.

SON: The social pulse of this city has been beating quite freely of late. Party-givings are numerous, party-goers are lively, and every person is gay. I have already formed the acquaintance of the young ladies of beauty and standing. It is a pity that I am not a more susceptible young man; although extravagantly fond of ladies' society, it appears that my admiration is too general, and not personal in its kind.

FATHER: Be careful, my son, how you visit young ladies in and about Savannah, or anywhere else.

MOTHER: I trust you have the bump of prudence well developed.

SON: On Thursday of this week a large fancy party was given at the residence of Miss Waring. It was a novel thing to me, and the evening was delightfully spent: a plenty of good cheer, good music, good dancing, and very many pretty ladies. There were costumes of every variety: ladies of the court of Louis XIV, French and Neapolitan peasants, countesses, queens, nights, mornings, seasons, gypsy girls, and Shakespearean ladies. Among the gentlemen we had the Emperor Napoleon himself, counts, monks, friars, brigands, country crackers, Turks, Greeks, and Arabs. Many of the dresses were magnificent, and the characters capitally sustained.... It is not a very easy matter to attend to business all day, prepare for the party at nine, be in attendance until an early hour, and then be prepared to resume your duties in the morning.

FATHER: Glad you are getting acquainted in a pleasant way with the good people of Savannah. But you are right to remember business and duty.

MOTHER: The world is not all pleasure.

SON: I am now prepared for admission to the bar, and wish that I could stand my examination, but will have to wait until the second Monday of May next.

MOTHER: My dear son, we hope to send you by the railroad tomorrow a nice roasting piece of beef, and a piece for steaks, which we hope will reach you in good condition.

FATHER: It will be placed under the care of Mr. Fulton, the conductor. If you do not receive it when the cars come in, you had best send to the depot and inquire for it.

SON: May I ask the favor of you, Mother, to have my summer clothes "overhauled," as the sailors would say? And when a suitable opportunity occurs, please send them to the city.

MOTHER: Can fine linen bosoms for shirts be got in Savannah? I have eight shirts nearly done for you—all to the bosoms; but my eyes have failed so much I am not able to *tuck* as I once did.

SON: You are very kind, Mother, in having the shirts made; and by tomorrow's cars I send eight bosoms, which you will, I am sure, think quite neat. My measure around the chest is forty inches, around the neck about sixteen and a half or seventeen.... I find that the decay of time is leaving marked traces upon several shirts now in my drawer, so that the present of these new ones will be acceptable indeed.

MOTHER: I am sorry, my dear son, to announce to you the sad

failure of the watermelons. The hot suns and rains have destroyed the vines.

SON: The absence of this fruit in a warm climate is sincerely felt by all.

FATHER: Andrew has planted some late seed, and I hope you will yet have some.

MOTHER: It always did me good to see you eat them, it was with such a relish.

SON: Messrs. Ward and Owens have very kindly offered me the position of a copartner with them in the practice of the law, which, as you may easily imagine, I have accepted.

MOTHER: I need not say, my dear son, that your father and myself are very much pleased at the offer made and accepted.

SON: Tomorrow morning I expect to leave the city for Brunswick on professional business. This will be my first experience on the circuit.

FATHER: We find today's *News* confirming the copartnership.

SON: Have been trying to find a suitable house. The rents are enormously high in consequence of the tremendous taxes of our city; and most of the houses offered for rent are either at a figure too high for me or in such out-of-the-way neighborhoods that I would not inhabit them as gifts.... Will you please, my dear parents, keep George with you about the house, as I do not wish him to forget his training. I want him to acquire a *house look,* which you know is not the acquisition of a day. He may have to be my little majordomo in the fall.

FATHER: This is the year to give blankets to our people. Will you look at Mr. Lathrop's stock and request him to send us sixty-five?

MOTHER: Getting all together, Mr. Lathrop may give us a good bargain.

FATHER: Blankets from $1.25 to $1.37 apiece.

MOTHER: We have not yet determined what we shall do in reference to *that family.*

SON: Phoebe and Cash—?

MOTHER: Phoebe and Cash—*and* their family.

SON: All five of them?

MOTHER: All five of them—Jane and Victoria and Cash Junior and Prince and Lafayette.

SON: I am very sorry that it will be necessary—

MOTHER: They have always been unprincipled. Jane gives constant trouble. Much as I should miss the mother, I will not separate them if I can help it.

SON: Thus far I have found Lafayette to possess uncommon intellect and faithfulness for a boy of his age; and it is not without feeling that I part with him. But it would be inhuman to separate the little fellow from his mother, and you are at perfect liberty to dispose of him with the rest.

MOTHER: It is a painful and harassing business.

SON: Will you oblige me, Father, by sending George here as soon as he conveniently can be spared?

FATHER: Your mother, not anticipating your early call for George, is obliged to keep him a few days to fix up his wardrobe.

SON: Hope that my sending for George will not inconvenience.

FATHER: He will be down, God willing, on Monday next.

SON: I am very much obliged to Mother for her kindness in having him fitted for his city entrée.

MOTHER: George has been a good boy.

FATHER: He is a smart boy, and I am glad you have one of his age so capable and reliable.

MOTHER: He is at the age when boys white and black require steady control and good influences and regular employment.

FATHER: Do, my son, require him to attend the Sabbath school and church.

MOTHER: He has a good memory and understands well.

SON: George has been at my heels ever since his arrival. He is considerably bewildered; says so many roads turn off he cannot keep the path; says he lives at "Miss Abby Jones's corner" (corner of Jones and Abercorn). I send his passage money (one dollar), which it entirely escaped my mind to send before asking you to commit him to the care of the conductor.... What did you think of the personal appearance of my majordomo? His garments fit him admirably, and he emphatically looks a little Corporal Trim. He expects to excite by his fine raiments quite the jealousy of his own sex, and the admiration of the fair sex of kindred extraction.

DAUGHTER: You cautioned me in your last letter not to omit returning answers to all of your inquiries. Now, I feel I can to *some* but not to *all*. I can give name and residence, but I am doubtful as to a full description! ... His name is the Rev. Robert Quarterman Mallard, a Presbyterian minister. Does that meet your approbation? He is settled in Walthourville, a village located in this county.... And now for his appearance. He is above medium height; has black hair and dark complexion; some say handsome, but I do not think so. And now I won't tell you anything more! ... I do not exactly know when the consummation will take place, but whenever it does I want to have you present. Cannot you be one of my attendants on that occasion?

SON: Yesterday afternoon about six o'clock Jane was arrested by Jones, a constable of this city, and is now in confinement in Wright the broker's yard.
MOTHER: Jane....
SON: She has been in Savannah more than a month, and is known by the name of Sarah.
MOTHER: Sarah....
SON: She was arrested in the house of Mrs. Dunham, a sister-in-law of old Mr. William Dunham of Liberty County.... About a month since, Mrs. Dunham was in want of a house servant to act in the capacity of chambermaid, and requested Nelson, Dr. West's house servant, who had a wife in the yard, to see if he could not get a woman whom she could hire to do the work. On the following day Nelson brought Jane (or Sarah, as she called herself) into the yard to Mrs. Dunham. Jane represented herself as belonging to a gentleman in the up country who allowed her to find work and pay wages— a very common thing in this city. She declared herself able to do housework, and agreed to work for Mrs. Dunham for $6.50 per

month. Mrs. Dunham states that she behaved herself very well, but was greatly inclined to be lazy, and at times somewhat impudent in answering back when spoken to with reference to her work.

MOTHER: Savannah is the last place in the world for servants inclined to evil.

SON: Mrs. Dunham assures me that she was honestly deceived in the girl, and took her at her representations, not suspecting at all that she was a runaway. She also begged me to take no legal steps in the premises. I find upon inquiry that Mrs. Dunham is a very upright, good, easy old soul who would do no one any harm, hard-working and suspecting no harm in another. She was wrong, however, in hiring the girl without a written permit from her master to find an employer.

MOTHER: Oh, yes!

SON: There are, you may say, hundreds of Negroes in this city who go about from house to house—carpenters, house servants—who never see their masters except at pay day, live out of their yards, and hire themselves without written permit. This of course is very wrong, and exerts a most injurious influence upon the relation of master and servant. Such a person did Mrs. Dunham think she was employing, and thus was deceived.

MOTHER: Deceived indeed!

SON: I told Mrs. Dunham under the circumstances I would institute no legal proceedings against her, and I had no doubt but that when informed of the facts you would sanction my course.

FATHER: I agree with you, my dear son, that no legal steps be taken in the premises.

SON: It is a question with me, Father, whether Jane should be allowed to come on the plantation again. Her tales of Savannah and of high life in the city would probably not have the most beneficial effect upon her compeers. But of this you will judge.

FATHER: She is no more to return to the plantation nor to the county. Her family out here are privy to her movements, and are in good spirits, and consider her gone for good. They will not be informed of her arrest.

MOTHER: We have concluded to dispose of the whole family, but not in Savannah nor in the low country.

FATHER: They must be sold up the country, where they will not come back.

MOTHER: It is very painful, but we have no comfort or confidence in them, and they appear unhappy themselves—no doubt from the trouble they have from time to time occasioned.

FATHER: Here is a list of them—to which Titus is added—with your mother's estimate, which cannot be far from a correct one. (*He reads.*) Cassius Senior. Father. Aged 45. Good field hand, basket-maker, and handy at jobs. $800. (I put him at that; Mother thinks it too low.) ... Phoebe. Mother. Aged 46. Accomplished house servant in any and every line: good cook, washer and ironer, and fine seamstress.

MOTHER: $1,000.

FATHER: Cassius Junior. Son. Good field hand. Age 21.

MOTHER: $1,000.

FATHER: Jane. Daughter (in town). Age 19. House servant, good seamstress, and field hand.

MOTHER: $900.

FATHER: Prince. Son. Field hand. Handy fellow. Age 16.

MOTHER: $800.

FATHER: Victoria. Daughter. Age 14. Smart, active field hand.

MOTHER: $800.

FATHER: Lafayette. Son. Age 12. Smart, active boy.

MOTHER: $800.

FATHER: Titus. Man. Age 29. Field hand and good oxcart man.

MOTHER: $600.

FATHER: Total: $6700.

MOTHER: All Cassius and Phoebe's family with themselves have excellent constitutions and are in good health.

FATHER: You can copy the list, my son, without the sums annexed and show it to Wright, and if you think best to Montmollin also, and learn what their estimate would be, and if they have orders from the up country, and could dispose of the whole family to one owner; for we cannot consent to separate them.

MOTHER: If the thing can be done, we will close the matter at once.

FATHER: Should you hear of anyone willing to purchase, you might come to some understanding about it.

MOTHER: Make no final contract without consulting us.

SON: Will you be good enough, Father, to send me a draft for the money to be paid as a reward to Jones, the arresting constable. You will remember the reward offered was twenty-five dollars. Jones told me he had been at an expense of fifteen dollars' spy money, and had had much trouble in watching an opportunity to arrest her. Whether you can believe a tale of this kind is a matter of great doubt. These constables are themselves notorious rascals. It would not be amiss, I think, Father, to give him thirty dollars, as rewards are running quite high.

FATHER: I think your idea a good one about the contable's fee; and I send you a check for thirty dollars payable to yourself which you can endorse and pay over to him and take his receipt.

DAUGHTER: I am truly sorry to find that there is a prospect of my being disappointed in regard to your being with me in April. If you do not come this time, I shall still hope this pleasure will be realized at some future day.... I have one favor to ask of you. Would you look in the Philadelphia directory for the name of Martin Gaul—G-A-U-L—and send me his direction. He married Miss Mary Carroll, a friend of mine.... Have the Misses Gill all left Philadelphia? What is their direction? Also Maggie Wilson's? And Sue Dickson's? And Lizzie Paul's? You can easily divine my reason for asking these questions. The 22nd of April is *the* day, and when my friends are invited, I do not wish to forget my Northern ones.

SON: Politics now forms the all-absorbing topic in our city. Both parties are sanguine, but it requires nothing less than a prophetic vision to foresee the result of the election.

FATHER: Buchanan's prospects seem by no means as encouraging as they were at first.

SON: The union of the Fillmore and Frémont men in Pennsylvania will, it is seriously feared, cause the old Keystone State to deviate from her hitherto unshaken adherence to Democratic principles. What a shame it will be if she repudiates Buchanan, her noble, trueborn son, for such a miserable offspring of fanaticism as Frémont "the Pathfinder"!

FATHER: The Union, in the event of Frémont's election, will, at least in this section of the state, be decidedly below par.

MOTHER: Disunion sentiments are already entertained to a very general extent.

SON: Our country was probably never before to such a degree disturbed by factions of a purely sectional character.

MOTHER: To what this will all lead, time only will reveal.

FATHER: It is to be sincerely hoped that every true lover of his country, of the liberties guaranteed under the Constitution, will come to the rescue.

SON: The other evening, returning home, I observed two sable sons of Nigritia in close confab beneath a lamp in the streets. As I passed I heard a short political dialogue, during which the profession was mutually made that they were "Know Nothings." I thought: "Surely for once we have proof that profession and practice are not always at variance!" If Negroes are talking politics in the streets, you may imagine to what an extent the whites are engaged.

MOTHER: The election has ended well.

FATHER: May it be the first act of divine goodness in our deliverance from the political and religious heresies which have been disorganizing and destroying the country!

MOTHER: For at least four years, under the administration-elect, may we hope for peace and prosperity.

SON: Beyond that period we scarce dare expect a continuance of our present relations.

FATHER: Buchanan and Breckinridge are elected, and owe their election to the South mainly; while the vote of the North with but few exceptions has been cast for Frémont.

SON: The next issue will doubtless be purely sectional. The

prospect is fearful, but everything indicates such a future condition of affairs. And when it does come, we of the South must and will be prepared to meet it bravely and without concession.

FADEOUT

Act Two

As the stage lights come up, the MOTHER *is seated on a sofa, doing needlework.*

MOTHER: Old Father Time is making rapid strokes from the grave of 1856, and hasting to welcome the light of a newborn year. Amid the hurry and cares of life I would gladly pause and with Memory's lamp linger amid the fading shadows of the past.... A happy, happy New Year to you, my beloved child! And should it bring over your life changes of vast importance, may they be only those of increasing happiness and usefulness!

SON: A Happy New Year to you both, my dear mother and father, with many pleasant returns! The old year passed gloomily away, and no sunlight dawned upon the morning of the new. The 1st was nevertheless a merry day in Savannah. The streets were filled with numbers on foot and in vehicles of every description, paying their New Year visits in obedience to what is now a well-established custom. Being in Rome, I would not be found negligent of Roman manners, and consequently "went the rounds," accomplishing in the space of some five hours and a half forty or fifty "pop calls." The ladies were all in pleasant humors, ready to receive; and the day was delightfully spent. Thus—for the present, at least—I am square with all the good folks in Savannah. To make amends for the day's amusement, after a late dinner I repaired to the office and there remained, pen in hand, until eleven o'clock.

MOTHER: As the captain of the *William Totten* was just loading for Savannah, I hastened Gilbert over with a bag of red potatoes for you, my dear son, sending also the money for the freight. But

Captain Charlie returns it, saying that "you are too good a friend for him to think of charging you." And he promises to send them safely as soon as he arrives.

SON: The red potatoes will be a great treat, and I hope that my generous friend Captain Charlie will not tarry too long in Romney Marsh.

MOTHER: Make Sue roast them in hot ashes; they are so much better than cooked in any other way.

SON: I send you, my dear parents, a little volume by the author of *Two Years Before the Mast,* which, giving as it does some interesting views of Cuba, may afford you pleasant occupation for an after-dinner hour.

FATHER: We are much obliged to you for the treat of Dana's *To Cuba and Back.* I read nine chapters to your mother last evening.

MOTHER: Dana describes finely; he paints. And one feels that he has taken a voyage to Cuba and seen the island himself.

FATHER: His *Two Years Before the Mast* is a capital work of the kind.

SON: I am happy to know that Dana's little book gave you so much pleasure. Dana is the only abolitionist for whom I ever entertained any profound respect. While in Cambridge I frequently saw him and often had occasion to admire him, not only as a lawyer and a scholar but also as a gentleman and a man of high-toned feeling and honor. His conduct during the Burns trial, and upon the occasion of the impeachment of Judge Loring, I will ever have cause to remember.

MOTHER: Please, my dear son, send us without fail on Saturday by Sandy Maybank, who comes out on the railroad on that day, ten pounds of best butter, for which I send a bucket, and one box of adamantine candles. Please see that these are a clear, white, and firm article. The last box sent us from Savannah was very inferior.

SON: By Sandy you will receive the ten pounds of butter and the box of adamantine candles. The butter is the best that can be had in the city—pure Goshen. The candles are perhaps not so white as you may have anticipated, but Mr. Goodrich assures me that no better article can be had; that they have given universal satisfaction, and burn evenly, brightly, and cleanly.

FATHER (*speaking directly to the audience, taking them into his confidence*): We are now in deep affliction. Our faithful old friend and servant Jack is no more. He was taken with the prevailing cold two weeks ago. A dreadful ague came on in the night; Dr. Way came a little after daylight and bled and relieved him; and for forty-eight hours everything went well with him. And then he took a turn for the worse. On Sunday hope began to give way, and on Monday all was gone; and last night—or rather this morning at half-past two o'clock—he passed away from us; and we have now nothing of the good, faithful old man but his cold body sleeping placidly in death, his countenance wearing that smile of life which you remember was so natural and constant with him. I was with him night and day, and am worn down with anxiety and watching. Almost every dose of medicine and every spoonful of nourishment he took from my hands. It is a heavy stroke to Mary and myself and the children. Jack was one of the family. I know you will sympathize with us and shed a tear for the old man.

But oh, how happy was his deathbed! Not a murmur; a smile for everybody; his mind clear and stayed on the Saviour to the last! He expressed himself ready to depart. He told his mistress "he was in God's sight but a filthy rag," but "his hope was in Jesus." He told me "it was a blessed thing to have a good master and a good mistress"; that "he could not begin to speak of God's mercies to him."

Seeing that he was failing on Monday morning, I had all the family called, white and black. And as each one came up, he took him by the hand and commended him to God. His reception of Charles was affecting. He was very fond of him, and when I said: "Jack, here is Charles," he reached out his hand and said: "Oh, my young master, this is my whole heart!" He was very affectionate to his mistress; he said to her: "I am so sorry to leave you; I know how you will miss me." We then prayed with him. Whenever religion was mentioned, a smile would come over his countenance. Indeed, it seemed as if the sun shone on his dying bed all the time, and suffered no cloud to rest there.

He gradually grew weaker from Monday morning till Wednesday morning, when, as I say, he died between two and three o'clock. Dr. Way had insisted that I should not sit up, and so Mary and myself arranged everything. Charles took charge of the medicine, and sent it out at the proper time to faithful men whom we had got to attend upon him; and when he died they carefully laid him out; and he now looks like one asleep who has a pleasant dream.

It is a sad loss to us—not only of a faithful, excellent, long-tried servant but of a devoted, long-tried, affectionate friend. And then there were so many thousand associations with Jack. He was a link that connected us with the past—with many of the beloved ones now dead, and with all the living. My dear wife feels it deeply. As I went down to dinner today, and he was not in his place by the table, but was lying dead in the servants' house in the yard, the tears came full and fast and fell down on the tablecloth; and I could not see the knife I held carving in my hand, and gave my seat to Charles and begged my dear wife to ask a blessing! We expect, God willing, to bury him tomorrow morning at ten.

Jack made a great impression on all who knew him, white and black. He was universally respected. For fifty years the old man has been very punctual in all his duties, and very attentive to religion, and has been ripening for his end. The Sermon on the Mount and the 3rd Chapter of John were favorite portions of his Testament which he used most frequently to read—though he was not a fluent reader.

The hand of the Lord is heavy upon us. But we would remember His mercies still. We derived much consolation from reading last night at family worship the first two chapters of Job. How hard it is for us to bring ourselves to believe in our own approaching end, and to resolutely prepare for it! Pray for us, and for our dear children, that we may all be sanctified and saved in Christ Jesus our Lord.

MOTHER: Sabbath was a cold, rainy day; we did not go to church. About one o'clock all the people large and small assembled in the vacant upper chamber, and your father gave them a practical discourse with the usual services. I have always delighted in the work of teaching the Negroes.

FATHER: The amount of ignorance among the Negroes is great, and I am surprised how little our own people seem to know of the Way of Life.

MOTHER: I wish every one of them had access to the Bible; it would much relieve our responsibility.

FATHER: What can be done for the better religious instruction of our Negro population?

SON: Jane is still in safe custody and well. Very few purchasers in the market. Two from Southwest Georgia last week would make no offer without seeing the Negroes. If they are to be sold, Father, in this market, they will have to be sent to Savannah.

FATHER: I thought, my dear wife, we had determined to part with the whole family, and were only waiting a month later for a better sale, until you appeared to hesitate on account of the trouble that would ensue upon the loss of an efficient house servant and seamstress. Our determination to sell the whole family was based, I believe, on these considerations: First, an indisposition to separate parents and child. Second, the unreliable character of the family. Third, in case of the sale of the present incorrigible runaway, Jane, apart from her family, although they have sent her away never to return, the effect upon them in all probability will not be for the better. And lastly, a change of investment would be more desirable than otherwise.... I do not wish to influence you in the least degree beyond your own convictions, nor to have you subjected to any inconvenience whatever in your domestic arrangements; and therefore I cannot assume the sole responsibility of a decision.

MOTHER: It is the second or third time we have had it in contemplation to sell this family.

FATHER: The sale of one may prove beneficial to the character and subordination of those that remain.

MOTHER: Time only can show.

FATHER: If not, they may be sent after her.

MOTHER: Certainly both she and her parents have settled the

matter, so far as they could, of her final removal from us and them; and it would be no special injustice to let her go.

FATHER: They could, I am certain, have brought her back, and they did not.

MOTHER: And they have sold all her clothing, plainly intimating that she is no more expected or desired back.

FATHER: Had she or they cause for all this, I should feel differently.

MOTHER: But I think they have not. Jane has been treated as our other servants have been, and every effort has been used to reclaim her—and without effect.

FATHER: If you wish the whole family sold, I have not the least objection. If not, then Jane may be sold and we may wait and see the effect. If for good, we shall be glad; if for evil, then we must meet the evil as best we may.

MOTHER: But I have very little hope of any improvement.

FATHER: Still I am willing to keep Phoebe and do all I can to make her profitable to you—as much so as in times past.

MOTHER: The main objection to the sale of the family, so far as I can see, is the loss of the services of Phoebe, who has given us more trouble, and even now and always has required more watching, than all our servants twice put together.

DAUGHTER: My eyes were quite refreshed by the sight of your well-known hand, though it did look rather queerly directed—to Mrs. Mary S. Mallard instead of to Miss Mary S. Jones.... We all regretted exceedingly your not being able to come to my wedding. Matilda Harden and my friend Kitty Stiles were my only attendants. My dear father performed the ceremony; and Brother Charlie and the Rev. Mr. Bowman were groomsmen; and the company generally seemed to think we were a pretty respectable-looking party.... Last Monday we went to Dorchester to see Mr. Mallard's parents. They received me very kindly, and I had a very pleasant visit, though I did feel rather awkward for a time, as I had never been in their house before. His mother asked me some funny questions, and if you will promise not to tell, here they are. "Mary, do you know how to keep house?" I told her no. Sometime afterwards she was speaking of sewing, and asked me if I knew how to make a vest, and I said, "No, I know nothing about making gentlemen's apparel." She did not question me further.

SON: Never before has Savannah witnessed such funeral honors as those paid on Monday last to the memory of the late mayor, Dr. Wayne. All day long the large flag at the city hall hung drooping at half-mast. As the procession moved from the late residence of Dr. Wayne to Laurel Grove Cemetery, all the bells of the respective churches united in tolling the solemn farewell. At the grave the usual Episcopal burial service was read by Bishop Elliott, after which the peculiar ceremonies of the Odd Fellows were performed around the open grave.... But to me, my dear parents, by far the most affecting incident was the singing of the Negroes in the cemetery. All the members of the choirs of the various colored churches in the city had taken position along one of the principal avenues. As the procession entered, they commenced singing that solemn funeral hymn, "We Are Passing Away." All the parts were admirably sustained, and there was a depth of feeling, a harmony, a propriety in voice and manner, that rendered the tribute exceedingly touching.

MOTHER: If it be dreadful to have the cry of the poor and the oppressed rising up to God against us, how sweet like incense poured forth their tributes of gratitude and affection!... One of the precious recollections of my own dear mother was her unvarying kindness to the poor and needy, which to their dying day embalmed her memory in their hearts.

SON: Adeline arrived last evening by the Savannah, Albany & Gulf Railroad, looking remarkably well and in fine spirits. She will, I hope, make us a good cook and a faithful servant. Sue's health was so bad that we were obliged to this arrangement. It makes us sad to part with Sue, she is so faithful, so honest, so respectful, so careful of the interest of her superiors, and so much attached to us. But she should leave Savannah. Dr. West says her days will be materially shortened if she remains.

MOTHER: It is a fact that persons liable to attacks of asthma cannot live with any comfort or health in Savannah.

FATHER: My dear son, Mr. Joseph Jackson has been engaged to take Cassius and Phoebe and their family (five in all) to Savannah on Monday, Providence permitting. Stepney goes down with him with the jersey and two horses—to divide the load and expedite the journey. They will carry provisions for the horses, and Jackson says he will put them in a yard and feed them where he usually stops, and they will be safe and at a trifling expense. Stepney will stay in your yard for the night, and will leave with Jackson on Tuesday morning for home.

MOTHER: On reflection we thought this the least public way and most speedy.

FATHER: Have directed Mr. Jackson to call at your house on his way in, and you would go around with him and see the people located.

MOTHER: They have taken their own clothing, and can put on what they like and appear well. Mr. Wright must see to this.

FATHER: Montmollin's estimate for six, throwing out Lafayette, is an average of $725; including him, $707.

MOTHER: Titus is altogether excluded.

FATHER: Wright's estimate for six, throwing out Lafayette—his lower estimate—is $750 round; including Lafayette is $733. His higher estimate, throwing out Lafayette, is $791; including him, $771.

MOTHER: We will take nothing under $800 round for the six; and if Lafayette is added, it ought to make no difference: he ought to be reckoned in at the same rate.

FATHER: You can give Mr. Wright your views, and he can get more if he can. And let him consult you before he closes the sale.

MOTHER: We do not wish them sacrificed.

FATHER: You can advise us of any offers made, and give your judgment of them.

MOTHER: We have had a sad day of it, as you may suppose—the

first of the kind in our lives. We could not conscientiously part the family, and therefore send all.

DAUGHTER: Can you realize that I am a minister's wife, and am actually keeping house and trying to feel the importance of my station? Sometimes when I think of it I sit down and laugh heartily! Mr. Mallard generally spends his evenings with me and reads aloud, which makes the time pass very pleasantly. Our readings have been various of late: sometimes history, sometimes theology, interspersed occasionally with Shakespeare. . . . How I should like to see you in my own house! And I flatter myself you would enjoy a visit—especially at this time, as I am quite a novice in the housekeeping art, though Mr. Mallard declares we are getting on swimmingly, and as long as I can keep *him* convinced of this fact, I shall be quite satisfied.

SON: Mr. Jackson and Stepney arrived safely with the Negroes. I hope, my dear parents, that this matter will not be a source of anxiety, for you have acted in the only manner which would meet the demands of justice and at the same time preserve the order and discipline of the plantation. If this family had been allowed to remain, it would always have been a disturbing element. Mr. Jackson and Stepney informed me that they appeared to be perfectly content, and the only regrets which they expressed were about the articles which they were compelled to leave. It is useless to waste sympathy upon a family of this character.

FATHER: The original instruction as to the sale to be adhered to—that is, sold out of the city, all together, to one owner (not a speculator), and in the up country or Southwest Georgia. When sold, give a bond for titles, or make what arrangement you think best to this end. Draw the titles and send them out, and we will execute and return them. Deposit the proceeds to my credit in the state bank, and send certificate of same.

MOTHER: We would be glad of a speedy close to this trying business.

SON: Lafayette was very much affected when I told him of your determination to sell his family. He wept bitterly. I have given him liberty to go with his father and mother or stay with me. He says that he prefers staying with me. His father has always treated him in an unfeeling and cruel manner. I believe that he is an honest child and sincerely attached to me. He will be much freer from bad influences where he now is. His services are far more valuable to me than any amount of money which I might receive. For these reasons I will not force him to go, but allow him to follow the dictates of his own feelings.

FATHER: I would be very glad on many accounts, my dear son, if Mr. Wright could effect a speedy sale.

MOTHER: You did well in procuring the shoes, and I wish you would get of Mr. Lathrop striped Negro winter cloth: six and a half yards apiece, and three yards of cotton homespun apiece, and some buttons and thread, and have it given to them. Phoebe and Jane can make it up in a few days.

FATHER: I do not know what the price of this property now is, or is likely to be, and $800 round may be over the market value. You can see and let us know.

DAUGHTER: I entirely agree with you that housekeeping in the city is not worthy the name. It really is not—especially in Philadelphia. I think Philadelphia quite a paradise for house-keepers—provided they have a long purse!... Yes, I keep my own house. I visit the smokehouse *occasionally;* I also make my fingers acquainted with the ingredients of loaf bread; I undertake to whip eggs; I wash cups; I see that the servants thrust their brooms into dusty corners; I buy beef; I pickle cabbage and other vegetables, besides many other fascinating little amusements connected with this wonderful science called housekeeping. ... I believe you are skilled in the art of bread-making. I have made good bread too, but the other day I was too amused: I "set some leaven," and it rose three days after! I thought it a fortunate circumstance the satisfying of our hunger did not depend upon that loaf of bread.... I am not an experienced housekeeper, so any nice receipts you may have will be thankfully received. I use only those that have been proven by the experience of my friends.

MOTHER: Your father and myself think with you, my dear son, that if $4300 can be realized for *that family,* you had best close the bargain at once. Of course, as we are compelled to sell, we would like to realize their value, but are willing to let them go for less in view of selling all together. We are now much in want of funds to meet our liabilities in bank. I know that you will do the best for us in this matter.

SON: I mentioned that Lafayette had determined to remain with me. He has, however, changed his mind, and expresses himself anxious to go with his parents. I have accordingly determined to sell him.

FATHER: We prefer the Negroes sold at a distance. If that be an impossibility, then the next farthest distance; but not in Savannah, and as far from this county as possible.

MOTHER: We prefer the sale to be cash.

FATHER: Or if credit be allowed for one year, then the security must be ample, with a responsible city acceptance. This will put us in funds which we need, and save all the trouble of future collection.

MOTHER: One-half paid down at the least; two-thirds if possible. A credit sale, of course, should be for a larger amount than a cash sale.

FATHER: The expenses are large keeping the Negroes in town, and Mr. Wright's entire bill if sold now will not be far from two hundred dollars.

MOTHER: He may manage to keep them on hand long enough to make a good profit.

FATHER: If you can sell for $4000 clear of all expenses, do so at once.

MOTHER: It will be a relief to have the business closed; it has caused me great distress.

FATHER: My dear son, you have drawn out the bill of sale

"warranting the Negroes sound." Now, this I am not able to do, not having seen them for weeks; and can only do so at any time to the best of my knowledge and belief.

MOTHER: The purchaser must take the risk after the day of sale.

FATHER: We can go nothing beyond that day.

MOTHER: We sell what we honestly believe to be sound, but we give no warrant which allows of after abatements or reclamation.

FATHER: The matter occasions your mother a great deal of anxiety, and I am therefore very anxious to close it, and hope Mr. Wright will use his best exertions.

MOTHER: We are well aware you will do *your* best.

DAUGHTER: Let me offer you my sincere thanks for your beautiful present to my little daughter. The case containing the fork and spoon preceded your letter by two or three mails. Mr. Mallard opened the package and handed it to me, saying that one of my friends had sent me a Christmas present. But upon closer inspection we found the initials were M. J. M. and not M. S. M. It was very kind in you to think of our little baby. You promised to bequeath a spoon to her in your will, but I am glad you thought it proper to allow her the use of it during your life.... She has improved very much: she sits alone now, can boast of one tooth, and says "bow wow" when the dog barks. Mr. Mallard speaks of having her likeness taken to be sent to you; so one of these days when she is a bit older, you may expect to find her little face in a letter.

SON: I am in treaty with General Harrison for the sale of the Negroes.

MOTHER: General Harrison....

SON: He will make a good master, and is a gentleman of high respectability.

MOTHER: It is a satisfaction to know into whose hands they will pass, and to believe that they will be well cared for.

SON: He will give, I am led to believe, $4200 or $4250 for the six.

MOTHER: Ah....

SON: He will pay some $2000 in cash and the balance by note with good endorser, payable at twelve months with interest from date. The family sold as a family will not command as high a price as when sold separately. From all I can gather (and there have been a number of purchasers in the market) the present, if consummated, will be the most advantageous arrangement that can be made. General Harrison wishes Phoebe and Jane as house servants, and gives on that account a much better offer than any hitherto made. I do not think, after the delay already experienced, that there can be any objection to the purchaser or the terms of the sale. But of this you will judge.

FATHER: Your mother and I after consultation agree with you that the sale should be closed with General Harrison at the price named.

MOTHER: The endorser should be a responsible *city* endorser.

FATHER: I think a mortgage on the property would make the matter still more secure. I am thus particular because the property is all your mother's but one, and I would not like to run any risk about it.

MOTHER: The property is in trust.

FATHER: Your mother desires the mortgage if possible; but in the event of not being able to secure a mortgage, do not let that prevent the sale if you have undoubted security.

MOTHER: We now leave the matter with you.

DAUGHTER: I wish you could have a glimpse of our dear little baby's face peeping out of the beautiful bonnet you made for her! I put it on her a few evenings since and carried her to see Mrs. McCollough; and much to my satisfaction, she behaved like a little lady, although there were persons enough around—and talking to her—to have frightened her. I believe some of the good folks here think me quite notional when I tell them I am afraid to send my baby visiting; but I do not think it right or safe to send babies about, particularly when so young.

SON: I have at last effected a sale: $4500 cash, Lafayette included, making $642.85 each, expenses to be deducted. The best sale that could be effected at present. Some four hundred now in the market; money scarce and hard to be obtained. They have all been sold to one person—not to be separated, but to remain on his own farm in the vicinity of Macon.

MOTHER: Macon....

SON: General Harrison did not purchase; his offer in the end was not as advantageous.

FATHER: They have been sold as we desired, and of this we should be glad.

SON: I could, by separating them, have made the sale more profitable; but what is profit as a compensation for having interrupted natural affection, and sundered ties which at least in the eye of God are as sacred with the Negro as with those who stand higher in the scale of civilization?

MOTHER: Conscience is better than money.

FATHER: We are gratified to know that the Negroes will have the prospect of a good master.

MOTHER: We hope all parties may do well.

DAUGHTER: Our dear little baby is the merriest, noisiest little mortal you ever saw. She says a good many little words; "Daddy" is one of the last she has learned, and she is very fond of saying it on all occasions.... Not long since she was at Montevideo. Mother's dress had some purple spots which of Baby's own accord she thought flies; and when Mother would come near her, she would put her little fingers on the spots and say: "Shoo! Shoo!"... You ask if she has any companions. Not yet; but I should not be surprised if you heard of an arrival next April.

FATHER: Is this infamous slave trade to be tolerated in our state and in South Carolina? Did ever mortal simplicity deliver such a speech as Thompson puts in the *News* this week from a *Mr. Spratt* of the South Carolina legislature? He certainly belongs to the school of the smallest and most common fishes that swim the ocean.

MOTHER: And Thompson deserves a leather medal for his discernment.

FATHER: I am much disgusted with his ridiculous remarks on the slave trade.

SON: Thompson of the *News* is a drunken fool, and that is all I have to say either for him or his paper.

FATHER: Am happy to learn the *Republican* speaks decidedly against the slave trade.

SON: Sneed of the *Republican* pursues a proper course.

FATHER: Are there no good and true citizens who will oppose this matter in the prints?

MOTHER: What do the thinking and respectable portion of your community say of the matter?

SON: The tone of feeling in the city is to a great extent extremely at fault; and such men as C. A. L. Lamar run riot without let or hindrance. And this will continue until they are guilty of some flagrant outrage, at which the feelings of even their hangers-on, in obedience to the indignant voice of the community, will revolt.

FATHER: Lamar is a dangerous man.

SON: And with all his apparent recklessness a cautious one too; for he never ventures in the presence of any save those whom he may readily intimidate.

FATHER: The great difficulty in cases of this character is to obtain testimony sufficient to procure conviction.

MOTHER: Parties who are interested refuse to testify on the ground that the testimony which they would give would criminate themselves.

SON: The examination of persons charged with transportation of slaves from Africa was today concluded, and resulted in the accused being remanded to jail to answer at the next term of the United States court to the charge of piracy.

MOTHER: A happy termination surely—one which should call for rejoicing at the mouths of all humanity-loving citizens.

FATHER: My dear son, here is Cassius' account. I have delayed until we could sell his mare. Balance to his credit: $84.75, for which here is a check, the space left blank for the name to whom the check shall be paid. Insert the name of Cassius' master, to whom you will please send the account and check.

MOTHER: But first write to him to ascertain if Cassius and his family are still with him, so that there may be a certainty of Cassius' getting his money.

FATHER: Keep copies of your letters, and register the letter enclosing the check when you send it.

MOTHER: We must use every precaution to get his money to him.

SON: I write today to Macon to the purchaser of Cash and family, and so soon as the necessary information is received, I will remit the amount of your check, which I hope will reach the owner in safety. I will also send a copy of the list of articles and personal property sold, with the prices obtained.

DAUGHTER: Last week we had the pleasure of a visit from our old friend Mr. Newton Russell. He seemed quite pleased with our baby. He said his second child was a most interesting little girl thirteen months old, just beginning to walk and talk. He has a heavy sorrow in his first child, a son. He is now four years old and has never noticed anything, is unable to walk, is a mere skeleton. There is something wrong about his head. Mr. Russell said he had an injury upon it, and he had consulted many physicians to know if any operation could be performed. Some thought he ought to risk it, even if the operation destroyed the child; but this of course he could not do. From what he said I gathered there must have been some malformation or perhaps injury at the birth. (I have heard since that the child is an idiot.) I could but feel how very thankful we ought to be to our Heavenly Father for having given us a perfectly formed child possessed of a sound mind. It made me sad to hear Mr. Russell talk of his poor little boy.

FATHER: The Harpers Ferry affair proves to be more serious than at first it appeared to be—not in reference to the Negro population, for that had nothing to do with it; but in reference to the hostility of large numbers of men of all classes in the free states to the slaveholding states, even unto blood. There is a covert, cowardly, assassin-like heart in these men. Why do they not arm and come to the field in open day?

MOTHER: From the tone of the abolition press in the free states, both secular and religious, there is great sympathy for the prisoners at Harpers Ferry. Some go so far as to justify the act, and only condemn the time and manner of it!

FATHER: The whole abolition crusade which has been preached for thirty years *ends in the sword.*

MOTHER: I have never realized before that the malicious fanaticism of the North could extend to such organized and practical results. It is no longer a war of words.

FATHER: Some of the papers friendly to the South hope that the South will be forbearing and magnanimous! There is no place left for forbearance. The magnanimity of the South must not be exercised towards public criminals of the deepest dye, but towards herself in all her greatest and best interests, and towards our common country. Such sparks as these, struck to produce a universal conflagration, should be stamped out immediately.... These are my sentiments, and I believe they are the sentiments of every intelligent and truehearted citizen in the Southern states. If the conservative and loyal men of the free states, who we believe do now possess the power, are willing to rule down this spirit of treasonable and violent aggression upon an unoffending section of our country, we shall be most happy to see them do it. But if not, then let them know that the fortunes of the American republic are embarked in one vessel, and neither stem nor stern shall be broken up without damage and loss of the whole!

MOTHER: My dear son, your father's remarks are so perfectly adapted to the present state of affairs that I asked if a publication of them at this time might not do good throughout the country. He says if you think so, you are at liberty to do what you please with them.

DAUGHTER: I was rejoiced to receive your letter day before yesterday—the more so because I was spared the pain of writing you a regular scold. I had been intending to write and ask if you had entirely blotted me from your memory. I almost began to wonder if you had been in the region of Harpers Ferry, and thought perhaps you might be so occupied with the affairs of the nation that you had no time for correspondence.... Thank you for all your good wishes in behalf of my family. Family! Does not that sound oddly coming from me? But really I *am* becoming *quite* a matron!... Last spring a sweet little boy was added to our number. He made his appearance on the 27th of April, and is a noble little fellow; has been blessed with perfect health since his birth, and has a decided talent for sleeping.... Little Mary is delighted with her brother, and often amuses me by the motherly way in which she talks to him. "Laugh, sonny boy! You sweetheart, don't cry! See—Mamie right by you!" She is a child of great activity of mind, so that I have constantly to be on my guard; and she often gets into trouble. It is no easy matter rightly to control a child. Native depravity shows itself pretty often.... But I have taxed your patience too long with my discourse on my children; I forget they cannot interest others as they do me.

FATHER: Our political sky is very cloudy! My hope is that He who has so often preserved our country will again show us favor, unworthy as we are, and deliver us from impending evils and grant us peace.

SON: Local politics are running quite high for a small town. We are in the midst of an exciting canvass. I have refused to take any part as a candidate or otherwise, except in a general way, and to such degree as every citizen should interest himself for the good of the community.

FATHER: You have acted perfectly right in the recent political troubles in Savannah, and just what I should have anticipated from your good judgment and prudence. If you desire *place,* you can afford to wait for it.

SON: Matters are just at this moment all at seas. The main question is: Shall law and order prevail in our community?

MOTHER: In questions of right there is a conservative element in every community which may safely be depended upon.

SON: Under the present administration the Sunday ordinance has become almost a dead letter; the rum shops are filled with Negroes drinking at all hours of the day and night; gambling is rampant. We wish an effective mayor: a man of honor, principle, determination; not a man of straw, a nose of wax.

FATHER: Do order the triweekly *Morning News* sent to me; I wish to know how matters are going in the state.

SON: I will see that the triweekly *News* is duly sent.

FATHER: The *Republican* is below par, and is offensive in its politics.

SON: The *Republican* is indeed beyond all endurance.

MOTHER: I trust, my dear child, that you will take special care of your health until there is settled cool weather. Do be careful not to expose yourself to the hot sun or night air.

FATHER: Use your umbrella in the heat of the day.

MOTHER: I have often heard that in Savannah October is the most sickly month in the year.

SON: By today's papers, my dear parents, you will see that I have been elected mayor of the city of Savannah.

MOTHER: Mayor of Savannah!

SON: I must admit that the compliment of the election comes home with peculiar effect, conferred as it is by the city of my birth.

FATHER: It surely is no common honor for one at your age to be called to direct the interests of fifteen or twenty thousand people.

MOTHER: I feel that just at this time above all others in our national history special grace and wisdom and decision are needed by all our rulers.

SON: The board-elect and the new mayor were this morning "sworn in," and we have entered upon the active discharge of our duties.

MOTHER: You are perhaps the youngest mayor Savannah has

ever had; therefore you must so act that no man may despise thy youth.

FATHER: Elevation to station and influence involves a responsibility which awakens solicitude in the bosom of every right-minded man; and instead of inflation and self-sufficiency he is prompted to humility and watchfulness. And knowing the fickleness of popular favor, and how trivial events cast down those who seem to stand firmest, he will trust but little to it, and take his satisfaction in doing his duty and making himself useful to his friends and his country.

MOTHER: And such lose not their reward.

DAUGHTER: The spirit of enterprise has at length reached this place, and we now have a daily train of cars passing through this county, and in this village we are now enjoying the blessings of a daily mail. Quite an improvement upon the old arrangement, by which our mail was brought twice a week by a stage. I verily believe we prized papers more then because they were a greater rarity.

FATHER: Here is a letter received today which will be as great a surprise to you, my dear son, as it has been to us. The man Lilly, who writes from New Orleans, is evidently a Negro trader, and not the permanent owner of the Negroes!

MOTHER: Lilly says he bought them in Savannah. This was not the name of the man who appeared in the purchase, nor was New Orleans his home. Was it not a planter near Macon who bought for his own use and not to sell again? Here seems to be deception—a wheel within a wheel!

FATHER: So soon as you hear from the ostensible purchaser you will know more about it—should he answer your letter.

MOTHER: Do not let him know of Lilly's letter. He may request you to send him the money for the people. Do not do so. It will be a roundabout way, and they may never get it.

FATHER: All we wish to learn of him is how the game has been played. If we have been deceived by Wright and the purchaser, we have been deceived. We were endeavoring to do the best we could.

SON: This revelation confirms me in the hitherto unshaken conviction that no confidence whatever can be placed in the word of a Negro trader. It is the lowest occupation in which mortal man can engage, and the effect is a complete perversion of all that is just and kind and honorable and of good report among men.

MOTHER: Am truly sorry to learn the death of poor Jane!

FATHER: How soon, how unexpectedly has she been cut off—the cause of all that has been done!

MOTHER: Would that she had lived and died at home in peace with God and with the world!

FATHER: I have prayed for those people many, many, very many times.

MOTHER: I wish them well.

SON: Our city, since these recent frosts, improves in health. The summer absentees are returning, and business has received an upward impulse. Legal matters, however, are quite stagnant. The doubt as to what another month may bring forth in the political status of our country exerts its depressing influence. The election of Lincoln seems now almost a fixed fact, in view of the recent advices received from Pennsylvania and Ohio and Indiana. The Republicans claim New York by a clear majority of forty thousand. Should Lincoln be elected, the action of a single state may precipitate us into all the terrors of intestine war.

FATHER: I do not apprehend any very serious disturbance in the event of Lincoln's election and a withdrawal of one or more Southern states, which will eventuate in the withdrawal of all. On what ground can the free states found a military crusade upon the South? Who are the violators of the Constitution? Will the conservatives in the free states make no opposition? If the attempt is made to subjugate the South, what prospect will there be of success? Is not the right of self-government on the part of the people the cornerstone of the republic? Have not fifteen states a right to govern themselves and withdraw from a compact disregarded by the other states to their injury and (it may be) their ruin?... But may God avert such a separation, for the consequences may in future be disastrous to both sections. Union if possible—but with it we must have life, liberty, and equality.

SON: The telegrams announce the fact of Lincoln's election by a popular vote! South Carolina has today virtually seceded. A meeting of the citizens here is called for tomorrow evening. We are on the verge of Heaven only knows what.

MOTHER: An indescribable sadness weighs down my soul as I think of our once glorious but now dissolving Union. Our children's children—what will constitute *their* national pride and glory? *We* have no alternative; and necessity demands that we now protect ourselves from entire destruction at the hands of those who have torn and rent and obliterated every national bond of union and confidence and affection.... When you were a very little fellow, we took you into old Independence Hall; and at the foot of Washington's statue I pledged you to support and defend the Union. That Union has passed away, and you are free from your mother's vow.

DAUGHTER: What cold weather we have had for several days past! This early cold always carries me back to Montevideo. Well do I remember the first fires that were kindled in the fall, and how we used to gather around the hearth—Father reading aloud, Mother knitting or sewing, Brother Charlie sitting upon the floor making mats with Taddy at his side; and I think I used to make mittens or sew my hexagon quilt. Father's reading was often interrupted by questions as to the probable time when frost would come; and if Daddy Jack made his appearance in the room, his opinion was sure to be asked.... We all have hearths of our own now, but I do not think any of them will ever burn as brightly as that one at Montevideo. There was always something peculiar about the first autumn fire....

FADEOUT

The Courtship of Carrie Davis

The Courtship of Carrie Davis is drawn exclusively from the letters of Joseph Jones (1833–1896) and Caroline Smelt Davis (1832–1868), written in 1859, and now preserved in the library of Tulane University (New Orleans).

JOSEPH JONES, *an attractive, intelligent young man in his twenties*

CAROLINE DAVIS, *an attractive, intelligent young woman in her twenties*

The scene is set in Augusta, Georgia, and Liberty County, Georgia, in 1859.

Act One

After the house lights go down, the voice of JOSEPH JONES *is heard in the darkness.*

JOSEPH: I have made the subject upon which I consulted you, my dear parents, one of careful meditation and earnest prayer. The intelligence, and charity, and piety of Miss Caroline Davis have completely won my heart. Two weeks ago I offered her my heart and my hand. Yesterday evening she returned a favorable answer.... I have been led to this step, my dear parents, by no motive except love. I have no more doubt of the sincerity of my own feelings, and of the worthiness of Miss Davis, than of my own existence. She is the idol of her family, and everyone who knows her loves her....

(*By now the stage lights have come up, revealing* CAROLINE DAVIS.)

CARRIE (*luxuriating in a box of chocolates*): My dearest Doctor Joe! I should like to think that all of your prescriptions are as agreeable as the one you've just sent me. I shall take it without making one wry face. Although you have no great respect for the French language, I must quote one of my little phrases: *"J'adore les bonbons, moi."* Is not that a real French superlative? ... And now the flowers! The flowers have just been brought to me, *mon plus cher,* looking just as lovely as anything possibly can. I have a special fancy for pinks: they are like the very breath of spring. Dearest Joe: you will accept *mes remerciements* for this flowery substitute for your presence. ... *But* you heartless, unfeeling man! You deserve to suffer something great for sending out your messenger into the pitiless pelting of such a storm as this evening. Don't you remember that line in

Lear: "Mine enemy's dog, though he had bit me, should have stood that night against my fire"? And you, a Christian man, send out poor Titus, the bishop of Crete, the emperor of Rome, "a man and a brother," with messages and tokens to an absent friend of yours! What would the abolitionists say? I have a great mind to send on your case to my connection, Mr. Gerrit Smith. Darling Joe: you really must not forget that the merciful man ordereth his household mercifully.... And now, having finished my tirade, I shall wind up by telling you how every line of your letter seemed pleasanter to me, how every word of it shone brighter to me, from having been written in the midst of clouds and sent out to me when I was just thinking the storm was going to last all night and I could not hope for any communication from town.... There—I will not detain your Mercury any longer. I quite tremble to think what a scolding you are going to give Titus the Roman emperor.... Do you know, I feel perplexed how to subscribe myself in closing a note to a gentleman.

JOSEPH: I might be perplexed when writing to a stranger, but never when writing to—a friend.

CARRIE: Shall I say, "Yours very truly"? Shall I say, "Yours respectfully"? Shall I say, "Yours sincerely"? Take whichever you like. At all events, good night, my—my— What would you like me to call you?

JOSEPH (*smiling*): Ah....

CARRIE: Tell me sometime, and if I feel very good and very pleasant, perhaps I will say it after you.

JOSEPH: I will expect you to keep your promise.

CARRIE: But you won't tell me what to say! And you know I only promised to say it after you!

JOSEPH: My dearest Carrie—good night.

CARRIE: Then I won't call you anything!... But I *will* say what I believe I've not said before.

JOSEPH: Ah....

CARRIE: I'm afraid it's not in your favorite language.

JOSEPH: Not in English?

CARRIE: It's in—French.
JOSEPH: Yes?
CARRIE (*hesitating*): It's only two words.
JOSEPH: Two words....
CARRIE: Two *little* words.
JOSEPH: Two *little* words....
CARRIE: Two *tiny* little French words.
JOSEPH: Yes?
CARRIE (*out with it at last, but whispering*): Je t'aime. (*More audibly*) Je t'aime.
JOSEPH (*pleased, touched*): Dearest Carrie—
CARRIE (*confidently*): Je t'aime.
JOSEPH: You are very, very precious to me, my love—dearer than all the world besides.
CARRIE (*delighted, almost in tears*): Oh, Joe!
JOSEPH (*in a crescendo*): You are my darling, my beloved, my spouse, my guiding star, my guardian angel, my pearl of great price, my spirit of light and love and truth, my—
CARRIE (*touched, amused*): Oh, my dearest Don José!
JOSEPH (*continuing the crescendo*): My morning star of hope! My evening star of peace! (*Commencing a decrescendo*) My own dear, dear love! My own dear, dear heart! My own dear, dear Carrie!
CARRIE: Darling Joe, no multiplication of epithets can intensify what you know I always feel.... I think, though, I shall have to give my favorite professor some lessons in the language.
JOSEPH: Lessons in the language?
CARRIE: How do you know how my head may be turned by such compliments, such comparisons—such amorous comparisons too? You know, those things depend entirely upon the person from whom they come. And I have been making such indiscreet admissions that it's rather late now to draw back from them and intimate the possibility of my *not* being a good deal moved by your pretty speeches. You are a dear, darling, good man. If it were not that I have some compassion upon that "downtrodden son of Africa" (poor Titus) I would go on writing till midnight. There—I

shall not write another word.... But, dearest Joe, are you quite worn out? I'm afraid those miserable students and their miserable examinations will tell heavily upon you this week. I was just going to say if you are too tired to come out on Saturday you must not make the exertion. But upon consideration I will not say it. I flatter myself that it will *rest* you to come out and see me.

JOSEPH (*playfully*): Ah, I call *that* vanity!

CARRIE: If all those pretty things you've been saying to me are true, it's but a fair deduction.

JOSEPH: If there is any spot on earth where I look for rest and happiness, it is where you, my love, dwell.

CARRIE: And by the way, I mean to let all the pretty speeches come from *you* in future.

JOSEPH: From me?

CARRIE: My face burns at the remembrance of those two little French words I spoke just now.

JOSEPH: Precious Carrie—

CARRIE: I thought it might be pleasant to you to have something to fall back upon—something to turn to—as somebody says, "The heart's sweet scripture, to be read at night when weary or at morning when afraid."

JOSEPH: "The heart's sweet scripture...."

CARRIE: But I didn't dream how those two little foreign words would send the blood flaming to my face just to say them.

JOSEPH: Dearest Carrie—

CARRIE: And I cannot—I cannot—say them again.

JOSEPH: Why should your cheek burn at the remembrance of a kind word? If you knew, my darling, how much joy such expressions give your love, you'd repeat them a thousand times.

CARRIE: I certainly hope my note reached you safely. It went down at the same time with one to Uncle William, and a dreadful fear has darted through my mind: suppose *he* got it instead of you!

JOSEPH: Uncle William....

CARRIE: What do you suppose he would think? I wonder if it would recall a time when *he* received notes on rose-colored paper with pet names scattered here and there, and foolish, fond fears expressed for his health.

JOSEPH: I should think it might call up ecstatic reminiscences!

CARRIE: Well, even so—I had much rather *he* should receive the kind, sisterly note Mother sent down with her little jars of jelly than have the benefit of that record of my feelings meant to be sacred from all eyes but yours. I shall not allow myself to *think* there was any mistake.

JOSEPH: When your sweet note arrived, I was sitting before my writing desk near a blazing, cheerful fire, and Puss was chasing a wicked mouse who had been making a bed of my books.

CARRIE: So Puss has returned at last!

JOSEPH: How shall I ever repay you, my love, for your precious letters?

CARRIE: I congratulate you upon the restoration of your cat.

JOSEPH: I wish I had words to tell you the hundredth part of the joy your letters always give me.

CARRIE: Do you think it was a late sense of gratitude for your last winter's kindness that brought Puss back to you?

JOSEPH: And many, many thanks, my dearest Carrie, for the charming paper. If *my* thoughts could only correspond to *your* paper, they would indeed be worth reading. But it is my misfortune, alas, to be a bad writer. So you must always read with the eyes of a sweetheart and not with the eyes of a critic. Just see how my lines run in every direction!

CARRIE: This afternoon Mother was in town and mentioned this *secret* of ours to my aunt, Mrs. Cumming. I suppose it *was* necessary; at any rate, Mother thought so. I did not like it myself; and as I thought of it, such a strange, uncertain, dim feeling came over me as to suppose it were not so at all. Was it *really real?* Was Mother telling a thing that had no existence? You know, it *was* sudden and unexpected; it has mingled so short a time with the rest of my life that sometimes I wonder if something so separate from my former life and yet so engrossing to me now is perhaps only a dream.

JOSEPH: Dearest Carrie—

CARRIE: What would you have thought of the siege of questions and remarks and jests to which I was a victim this evening at the hands of Mr. Ganahl! Really, the audacity of his style was so remarkable that I was perfectly silenced. Among other things he told me that Savannah has been rocked to its foundations by the excitement into which it has been thrown by this important question. It *is* flattering, isn't it, to furnish interest to so many!

JOSEPH (*laughing as he reads letter*): "Mon trésor. Mon plus cher. Consuelo di mi alma—"

CARRIE (*laughing*): What it is to have a *sister* who exhausts every language of Europe for terms of endearment!

JOSEPH: A sister?

CARRIE: Of course a man of your discrimination would not suspect a reserved, undemonstrative correspondent like *me* of all that polyglot salutation!

JOSEPH (*continuing to read letter*): "Consuelo di mi alma. Amantissimus. Carissimus—"

CARRIE (*still laughing*): Here I was beginning in my usual grave, proper way when my pen was reft from my hand and all those caressing epithets put at the head of my sheet!

JOSEPH (*pleased*): My dearest Carrie—

CARRIE: Well, I hope you feel flattered by Sarah's pretty foreign words. She sends her love to you. And so does Julia. And so do I.

JOSEPH: Give my very best love to Miss Sarah and Miss Julia. And tell them that notwithstanding my silence and my cold exterior I think of them often, and love them as you love them, and have formed many bright visions of the future when they shall sparkle in *our* happy home.

CARRIE: Dear Joe, do you know, I and my sisters (bad grammar) —my sisters and I—want you to drop that objectionable *Miss* to their names: *Miss* Sarah, *Miss* Julia. Don't you think if you practiced it by yourself you *could* say Sarah and Julia?

JOSEPH: My dearest Carrie, may I have the pleasure of taking that delightful walk with you tomorrow?

CARRIE: Come out by all means tomorrow.

JOSEPH: If you say so, I will take an early breakfast and be with you about nine or half-past nine in the morning.

CARRIE: About half-past nine or ten will be early enough to start.

JOSEPH: Do you know, I have the greatest desire to take that walk and pluck wild flowers for my dearest Carrie.

CARRIE: It may be that we shall decide in council that it's not bright enough or dry enough to take that particular walk.

JOSEPH: I have thought of that walk ever since you spoke of it a month ago.

CARRIE: Be sure and be out here by ten o'clock. I shall expect you whether we're able to take the walk or not.

JOSEPH: You must not let me take you away from your sisters. If you prefer walking with your sisters, I will walk with you and your sisters. If you prefer to sit and talk with your sisters, I will sit with you and talk with your sisters.

CARRIE: Ah, Joe, we're all going to be so good to you, it's really sad to think how vain and inflated you'll become by the time you get back to your former friends!

JOSEPH: They'll find me quite insufferable, I know, and blame you severely for it all.

CARRIE: My dearest Joe, I *may* go on using that endearing epithet, may I not? Or would you rather I should choose some other? Do you know, we're all going to call you Joe hereafter—that is, Sarah and Jule and I. We've always had a fancy for the name, so if you don't want us to, you "must now speak," as they say in the Prayer Book, "showing just cause, or else hereafter forever hold your peace."

JOSEPH: By Titus, the bishop of Crete, I send you a few more flowers.

CARRIE: A few more flowers!

JOSEPH: They are much more beautiful than those from Liberty County.

CARRIE: Dearest Joe—

JOSEPH: I was really ashamed to send you such frost-bitten, commonplace flowers.

CARRIE: But, dearest Joe, they were charming!

JOSEPH: The only charm about those flowers was that they came from home, and were arranged by my sister.

CARRIE: Oh, do give my love to Mary when you write. And tell her I hope we shall indeed be dear sisters to each other.

JOSEPH: She's never had a sister.

CARRIE: That seems strange to me. I feel as if the happiness of my life has been the companionship of my sisters. I wonder if she will take me for a real sister.

JOSEPH: Do you know, you resemble my sister very much.

CARRIE: Indeed?

JOSEPH: In disposition, I mean. Like her you are a sunbeam.

CARRIE: A sunbeam....

JOSEPH: The sunbeam not only paints the landscape and reveals the exterior material world to the interior spiritual nature; it also produces a permanent impression upon the world's history.

CARRIE: A permanent impression....

JOSEPH: Not only the happiness but even the existence of all animated beings depends absolutely upon the force of the sunbeam.

CARRIE (*not fully comprehending this, changing the subject*): I had been wondering all day if I were not to hear one little word from my favorite professor before Saturday; but I had come to the conclusion it was not to be expected that a man plunged in all the excitement of preparing his fellow men to go forth and do battle in the great field of life and death should find a spare moment for writing a frivolous love letter; so I had resigned myself to it, trying to be comforted with the reflection that it was better to *expect* letters from you than to *receive* them from anyone else.

JOSEPH: Now, isn't *that* loyalty!

CARRIE: And so after a while the bishop of Crete brought me your letter.... *And* those superb flowers! I have just finished arranging them, and the parlor is a perfect Vale of Kashmir.

JOSEPH: Keep two or three to wear.

CARRIE: *But,* darling Joe, what a man you are, to be sure! I never saw anything like you! Is this the way you think flowers ought to be strewn in the pathway of your love? You're going to spoil me—after all my talk about spoiling *you.* The flowers are so beautiful—the azaleas so radiant, the roses so perfect, the calla so pure—no words *I* can use begin to express them.

JOSEPH: In the center of the flowers you will find one of snowy white which I have selected as a type of the beautiful image formed by the *sunbeam.*

CARRIE: Do you know, I'm afraid you're rather imaginative about that image of light. Suppose you should find someday that the sunbeam had not reflected truly—that the image was not as fair as you thought it.

JOSEPH: Not as fair?

CARRIE: It's a sad thing to destroy illusions, but I don't like to think that my friend may one day find that his sunbeam has been a false medium.

JOSEPH: A false medium?

CARRIE: You see, I think it the part of a friend to warn you. . . . Oh, how sweet the flowers! And how sweeter the remembrance!

JOSEPH: Dearest Carrie—

CARRIE: What begins to compare with the charm of knowing that my beloved thinks of me always, and expresses his thoughts in this most beautiful way! Don't you think you'd better stop before you spoil me completely? . . . But, dearest Joe, I am going to lay you under a ban: from this time on you are not to bring me or send me another thing. Don't forget, now: I am really in earnest. Not another thing!

JOSEPH: Dearest Carrie—

CARRIE: One reason I wanted to see you before Saturday was that I have had a ring engraved for you which will much better befit your hand than that striking ruby of mine.

JOSEPH: A ring. . . .

CARRIE: But perhaps it won't lessen its value if *I* wear it for a day or two.

JOSEPH: Precious Carrie—

CARRIE: The 18th of February was an eventful day for you and me, and I thought I would commemorate it with this little gold circle.

JOSEPH: Tell me, Carrie—have you quite forgiven me for not recognizing you that time?

CARRIE: I have quite forgiven you, and I should have told you so the other day but that I was sick—and as unlike a sunbeam as possible.

JOSEPH: I sincerely hope your cold is better.

CARRIE: My cold is almost gone, I'm pleased to say; but I've not quite shaken off that provoking cough.

JOSEPH: I have blamed myself for inducing you to take that long, cold drive.

CARRIE: I was not at all injured by the drive.

JOSEPH: The fact is, I was not aware that the sun had set, because I was enjoying sunbeams more beautiful to me than even those of the great source of light and life.

CARRIE: I did not increase my cold, but I *did* find quite a lecture waiting for me.

JOSEPH: A lecture?

CARRIE: And if you had not pursued the politic course of declining to come in, you would have shared it.

JOSEPH: You must think me a kind of evil omen!

CARRIE: All that I could say to stem the tide was that it should not occur again. So—you are committed either to starting earlier or to taking a shorter drive on Monday.

JOSEPH: In my rambles I have discovered a hill which commands the city and affords an extensive view of the surrounding country. May I have the pleasure of escorting you thither on Monday?

CARRIE: I will visit that commanding hill with pleasure—if it does not rain.

JOSEPH: I will be with you, my darling, on Monday morning. And if I am successful, I will bring you my likeness.

CARRIE: Your likeness!

JOSEPH: And you must give me yours.

CARRIE: I begin to think there's a fate against that likeness of me.

JOSEPH: I will take no refusal.

CARRIE: My own scruples threatened it for some time, and then when I had changed my mind, everything else conspired. I was sick yesterday, and today the weather prevented. Someday soon I shall try, solely out of consideration to your wishes; so you must appreciate it, for am I not risking a dreadful stab to my vanity just to please you?

JOSEPH: A stab to your vanity?

CARRIE: The worst kind, some people think it.

JOSEPH: And you must send me, darling, that lock of your hair.

CARRIE (*smiling*): Ah....

JOSEPH: But you must not spoil that splendid head of golden hair of which I am so proud.

CARRIE (*touched*): Oh, Joe!

JOSEPH: You know you promised to make it grow ever so long for me. (*Intimately*) When I am with you, will you not show me—how much it has grown?

CARRIE (*abruptly changing the subject*): Is not this a debilitating day!

JOSEPH: Debilitating?

CARRIE: It feels like one of those debilitating days in *May*.

JOSEPH: I see you do not like the month of May.

CARRIE: Alas, I do not like the month of May.

JOSEPH (*reading*):

> Now the bright morning star, day's harbinger,
> Comes dancing from the east, and leads with her
> The flowery May, who from her green lap throws
> The yellow cowslip and the pale primrose.
>   Hail bounteous May that dost inspire
>   Mirth and youth and warm desire!

> Woods and groves are of thy dressing,
> Hill and dale doth boast thy blessing.
> Thus we salute thee with our early song,
> And welcome thee, and wish thee long.

These lines from Milton are so ardent—so enthusiastic.

CARRIE: *And* so very beautiful.

JOSEPH (*reciting*):

> My beloved spake, and said unto me:
> Rise up, my love, my fair one, and come away!
> For, lo, the winter is past,
> The rain is over and gone;
> The flowers appear on the earth;
> The time of the singing of birds is come,
> And the voice of the turtle is heard in our land.

CARRIE: What an avalanche you bring down upon me from writers sacred and profane!

JOSEPH: But you do not like the month of May.

CARRIE: Do you know, I pride myself greatly upon my practical wisdom. But I fear you will doubt it when you know how invincible my aversion is to the joyous month of May.

JOSEPH: Aversion?

CARRIE: For a final leave-taking, I mean, to this dear delicious free life of mine.

JOSEPH: But, my dearest Carrie—

CARRIE: Wasn't it a terrible mistake in my education? But there it is—inwrought.

JOSEPH: My dearest Carrie, whatever pleases you will please me.

CARRIE: But human nature *is* sensitive to omens; and you, *mon bien aimé,* would not have anything but bright omens gather round that most important day of our two lives, would you?

JOSEPH: If you dislike May, why can't you make it—even sooner than May?

CARRIE: Darling Joe, I feel I must ask you for time.

JOSEPH: Time? More time than May?

CARRIE: Well, even the greatest minds have their little weaknesses. And this, it seems, is mine.

JOSEPH: Dearest Carrie—

CARRIE: Are you vexed that I dare state my own foolish superstition immediately upon hearing the words of Milton and the Song of Songs, when you might reasonably suppose that such poetry would have silenced anything so foolish?

JOSEPH: Dearest Carrie—

CARRIE: How shocked you must be to find traces of imperfection gathering! But you know I warned you.

JOSEPH: For my part I would be glad if we were even this moment united in the holy bonds of—

CARRIE: When I see you next we will talk it over again, and then I will tell you decisively.

JOSEPH: And meanwhile—?

CARRIE (*smiling*): Meanwhile it's on my mind day and night.

JOSEPH: Day *and* night?

CARRIE: If I had time—that is, if I had no compassion on that unhappy man of yours, the bishop of Crete—I would quote and counterquote until you would acknowledge that at least I had studied the subject as profoundly as you have.

JOSEPH: My own sweet Carrie, I hope you will choose the shortest possible waiting-period.

CARRIE: Dearest Joe, you who say you know me so well must know that your wishes go very far with me. They're *almost* my *law.* And soon they'll be *altogether* my law.

JOSEPH: Then it *will* be May.

CARRIE: If you really wish it—yes, it *will* be May.

JOSEPH: I am debating in my mind whether to spend the four months of vacation—June, July, August, September—with Father and Mother in Liberty County, where I will have an opportunity of prosecuting my researches with little interruption and at much less expense than in Augusta. I have an immense work before me: Southern diseases and plantation hygiene. If I enter into practice I will be compelled to abandon my investigations. And if I reside permanently in Augusta I will be compelled to enter into practice on account of the great expense of living.

CARRIE: Darling Joe, I was obliged to tell my sisters when they asked me that you had forgotten to send your love to them.

JOSEPH: Did I forget to send my love to your sisters?

CARRIE: They say they return good for evil and send theirs to you.

JOSEPH: It was not, I assure you, because I love them the less but you, my Carrie, the more.

CARRIE: What are you doing this evening? Writing? Correcting for the press? Reading some author who sprains your intellect as you take in *his* profundities? Do you find time to send a thought Hill-ward—just a little one—now and then?

JOSEPH: My dearest Carrie, whether I am writing or reading, sitting or walking, talking or keeping silence, waking or sleeping, your image is always before me.

CARRIE: If you've been keeping up your usual vigils beside all these extra labors, I fear you will be like that student famed in verse of whom it was said:

> Much study had made him very lean,
> And pale, and leaden-eyed.

Don't go and get too ethereal, now. And don't bend over your books too much. For though it may give you a scholarly appearance, you know I'm very tall, and if you're going to walk through life with so tall a woman as I am, you'll need all your inches.

JOSEPH: I promise to turn over a new leaf and not study so hard. And I will walk more erect, and strive to look better. I have someone now to care for.

CARRIE: I never asked you whether you liked height in women.

JOSEPH: My precious Carrie—

CARRIE: You know, I'm dreadfully sensitive about my height.

JOSEPH: You need never be sensitive, darling, on my account.

CARRIE: For a long time I refused to be comforted about it—until one day I found a line somewhere among my favorite poets (was it Tennyson?) describing

> A daughter of the gods, divinely tall,
> And most divinely fair.

JOSEPH: My dearest Carrie, you don't know how much I admire your height.

CARRIE: "Divinely tall": I'm not sure but it was put in just for the sake of rhyme, but at any rate it consoled me.

JOSEPH: My dearest Carrie, I would not have one line altered in your features, or your form, or your stature.

CARRIE: Oh, Joe!

JOSEPH: Could you ask me to say more?

CARRIE: Oh, Joe!

JOSEPH: Now, doesn't this letter deserve a little French? Or at least a little Saxon? I will not say how much; I will leave your noble and generous and loving nature to decide.

CARRIE: I have been writing too hurriedly to summon up my French. And pure old Saxon somehow seems to me unmaidenly. It makes me blush, so I don't think it can be right to use it. Now, that is a case of conscience for *you* to decide.

JOSEPH: Tell me, darling—do you feel you need rest after the fatigues of yesterday?

CARRIE: It would be much more appropriate if I asked *you*. After all *your* exertions physical and mental, are *you* not tired?

JOSEPH: I wish I could tell you how happy I was.

CARRIE: I'm so glad you enjoyed the day.

JOSEPH: You must not call me a flatterer when I tell you that yesterday was the most delightful day of my life.

CARRIE: *I* thought it charming.

JOSEPH: Why should it not have been? Was I not with my spirit of light and love and truth?

CARRIE: Now and then I *was* a little afraid you thought it rather a frivolous way of spending time you might have been employing for the benefit of the world at large.

JOSEPH: *But,* my dearest Carrie, was it altogether right in you to refuse that—that tiny little—manifestation of love prompted by a heart overflowing with love?

CARRIE (*ignoring the question*): Tell me—did your head ache after all that sun? It acted like mandragora to me; it "medicined" me to a charming nap on the sofa between the arduous exertions of dining and reading aloud to Father.

JOSEPH: My head did not ache.

CARRIE: Dear Joe, I'm afraid I did not look pretty in the woods yesterday morning.

JOSEPH: Not look pretty?

CARRIE: I think you were, as the French say, *disenchanté, n'est-ce pas?*

JOSEPH: I do not think as the French.

CARRIE: Remember: it was *your* fault that my hair came down and presented that—that picturesque appearance when it had to be put up.

JOSEPH (*smiling*): *My* fault?

CARRIE: Now, Joe—honor bright: the sun was *not* a flatterer, was he?

JOSEPH: My darling Carrie—

CARRIE: I never mean to take a walk with you again.

JOSEPH: My darling Carrie, you must believe every word I tell you, for you know that *I* am no flatterer.

CARRIE: Do you remember that Friday in February when I left you for a little while to change my dress for driving? I gave you a passage in Shakespeare to ponder during my absence. (*She recites.*)

> Though for myself alone
> I would not be ambitious in my wish
> To wish myself much better, yet for you
> I would be trebled twenty times myself,
> A thousand times more fair, ten thousand times more rich.

JOSEPH: Shakespeare always has a way of saying just what comes home to everybody.

CARRIE: Do you know, I never used to wonder whether I were pretty or not. But now it is perfect anguish to me to think of the possibility of losing what *you* value.

JOSEPH: Precious Carrie—

CARRIE: Dear, dear heart, you *will* go on loving me when I have ceased to be lovely even in your eyes?

JOSEPH: My dearest, dearest Carrie—you possess everything I love, everything I adore, everything I hold most sacred on this earth. I can never love you enough.

CARRIE: By the way, speaking of Shakespeare: didn't you tell me that you have an edition?

JOSEPH: Yes, I do.

CARRIE: Alfred Cuthbert sent me word that he considers Shakespeare essential to every household, and he has it in mind to bestow a set upon us.

JOSEPH: Ah....

CARRIE: But since you have one, I shall suggest something else.

JOSEPH: My dear Carrie, I send you a bunch of flowers which I hope will atone for the miserable one I collected for you yesterday.

CARRIE: Ah, Joe—how lovely!

JOSEPH: You promised me whilst I was displaying my "circus performance" in the pine trees that you would take the will for the deed.

CARRIE (*with a knowing smile*): "Circus performance"?

JOSEPH: I wished very much to send the flowers wet with the morning dew. But, alas, I have been interrupted and interrupted by calls from my professional brethren.

CARRIE: So you've been doing professional hospitality today!

JOSEPH: Two of them brought pathological specimens which they asked me to examine in their presence and explain.

CARRIE: I'm afraid you didn't feel altogether cordial at their interruption of your work.

JOSEPH: This afternoon I determined to visit you after the meeting of the faculty of the Medical College of Georgia. But, alas, the faculty continued in session—or rather continued to joke and laugh and talk in my office—from three o'clock to the present time: half-past seven. Four hours and a half! They were in my own office, and what could I do? I tried to console myself with the hope that they would leave in time for the preparation of a respectable *letter* to you; but even this consolation was taken from me.

CARRIE: And will you work until the small hours of the night? I *think* you have earned a long night's rest after your "circus performance."

JOSEPH: Look at the flower in the middle of the bunch. Do you know it was named after you?

CARRIE: After *me?*

JOSEPH: It is a very high compliment to the flower. I have yet to see any flower that equals the grace and beauty of *my* dear flower.

CARRIE (*touched*): Oh, Joe!

JOSEPH: You must take these flowers, my dearest Carrie, as the exponents of my deepest feelings. Notwithstanding my trembling hand and my stammering tongue, you know you possess my whole heart.

CARRIE: Do you suppose it's only on your side? My own beloved, my words are weak and insufficient; I can scarcely hope they give you that perfect satisfaction that yours give me.... *But,* darling Joe—*mon plus cher ami*—how disobedient you are!

JOSEPH: Disobedient?

CARRIE: Did I not tell you that you were not to bring me or send me another single thing? You thought I was not in earnest, but I was. Now, I am going to limit you each time you come up here. After these splendid flowers have had time to wither, you must bring me one single rose. Wear it out here, and when you come I will transfer it to my pin and will wear it until it fades. But if you bring me more than one, I will not have it. Now, do you hear, my dearest? I have said it. Just to think, these lovely flowers make the third you've sent me in one week!

JOSEPH: My dearest Carrie, I regretted very much that it was out of my power to see you today. I have allowed the bishop of Crete to go home for a few days and see his friends, and it was necessary to make arrangements for him at the railroad station.

CARRIE: Darling Joe, dearest Joe, sweetest Joe: do you think you could do me the greatest favor in the world?

JOSEPH: Carrie—

CARRIE: I will love you better than I ever did before.

JOSEPH: Carrie, darling—

CARRIE: I want you—if you don't think I ask too much—I want you to propose to Julia to drive with you instead of me.

JOSEPH: Julia?

CARRIE: She is so unwell she wants some such thing to revive her.

JOSEPH: Julia....

CARRIE: She would never consent if she thought I had asked you. But if you just *would* ask her—tell her you know I don't want to—I will give you a hundred kisses.

JOSEPH: Carrie—

CARRIE: And perhaps I may even put in a little French—if Saxon fails me.

JOSEPH: Carrie—

CARRIE: It will be a favor for which I will thank you forever.

JOSEPH: Dearest Carrie—

CARRIE: But don't say a word to *me* in answer.

JOSEPH: Dearest Carrie, I enclose a little note to Julia which you can read and seal and hand to her if you think best.

CARRIE: A note....

JOSEPH: If you are jealous, destroy it.

CARRIE (*laughing*): Jealous....

JOSEPH: Is not this being very respectful to my Carrie, to whom I belong?

CARRIE: Dear Joe—

JOSEPH: I also send you a paper containing a notice of my address before the state medical society in Atlanta. I am almost ashamed to send it, the commendation is so fulsome and undeserved.

CARRIE: You know I love to see such tributes—not because they add anything to my opinion, but it is delightful to me to know every meed of praise rendered to you.

JOSEPH: My dear Carrie, I have laid all my summer plans before Father and Mother. They think it would be running a risk for me to bring you down to the seaboard during the month of May.

CARRIE: Running a risk?

JOSEPH: You know, my precious one, that I would not upon any consideration jeopardize your health.

CARRIE: Joe—

JOSEPH: And this risk has led me to alter my plans somewhat.

CARRIE: Alter your plans?

JOSEPH: Would you be offended with me if our wedding should be deferred to a much later period than May?

CARRIE: Deferred?

JOSEPH: Would it not in fact be a great relief to you to avoid this dark, unfortunate, disastrous month?

CARRIE: Joe—

JOSEPH: I know that I acted in a very selfish and arrogant manner when I persuaded you against your own will and the earnest remonstrances of your family.

CARRIE: Joe—

JOSEPH: I know that I acted in a very selfish and arrogant manner when I persuaded you to resign your "dear free life" and leave your happy home and dear father and mother and sisters upon so short a notice, simply for me—a poor, lonely, selfish, arrogant man.

CARRIE: My dearest, I believe you acquit me of the folly of attaching any importance to that absurd superstition about May. But I have a feeling—a foreboding—that one such important change of an arrangement to which I consented entirely out of consideration for your convenience will be but the precursor of others.

JOSEPH: You know that your happiness will be the great object of all my arrangements.

CARRIE: Doubtless there are excellent reasons for the change. But I would give anything on earth if I had known it a few weeks earlier.

JOSEPH: I can make no arrangement that will not meet your entire approbation and promote to the very extent of my power your happiness.

CARRIE: I shrink with such a *shudder* almost from the remarks—the unbounded comment—that will arise. I have some courage, I think; but I *dread* the license of speech which so many have no scruple in using.

JOSEPH: I will make every effort to be with you as soon as possible and lay all my plans before you, my dearest and best friend.

CARRIE: Horrid man that you are, who would believe it of you? You're almost as bad as the man in the old records who wanted to put away his wife when he got tired of her!

JOSEPH: My love, you will do me a *great favor* if you will mention this contemplated change to no one, not even to your father and mother, until I have consulted your highest happiness in everything.

CARRIE: Ah, Joseph—I shall show you your last letter when you come out, and point out to you a number of frigid little expressions that were calculated to startle a trusting and confiding heart.

JOSEPH: I know that my letter was calculated to make you feel that I was cold and fickle. But God knows that this was not the state of my affections. I never felt more keenly any disappointment in my life. I did honestly reproach myself for having persuaded you against your will with reference to the month of May; and I almost knew that it would be pleasant for you to change the time back to October—the month you originally suggested. The preservation of your health was the *only* reason for a delay. You will believe me when I tell you that my father and mother and all my relatives would have been delighted to have you as one of their number this summer. At the same time Father and Mother asked me if I was aware of the risk of moving from Middle Georgia to the seaboard during the month of May. "Suppose," they said—"suppose she should be taken sick away from her mother and father and sisters? We would do all in our power to relieve her, but that would not relieve your mind if anything should happen." I determined to make any and every sacrifice rather than jeopardize your health.

CARRIE: My own, I would not if I could avoid it say one word to trouble you for the world.

JOSEPH: My beloved, I know that that letter looked cold. Oh, how it contrasted with *your* precious letter—notwithstanding that it contained a gentle but just reproof. How I hated to destroy that letter with its noble words of love!

CARRIE: I am very much obliged to you for burning my letter; I had reasons good for wishing it.

JOSEPH: You commanded and I obeyed: it was consigned to the fire.

CARRIE: I do not like to seem cold, and *you know* I am *not* cold. But I have been under the shadow of that undefined foreboding all day, and I suppose I have involuntarily communicated it even to this rose-colored paper.

JOSEPH: My dearest, you must not let those gloomy forebodings distress you. Trust in God. He will direct all things for our best good.

CARRIE (*changing the subject*): I did not think, *mon cher ami,* that you would have so coolly disregarded the very emphatic suggestions I threw out about my *willingness* (to use no other word) to have you spend last evening with us; but it seems you had something better to do and sent me no sign.

JOSEPH: My dear Carrie—

CARRIE: I could hardly bring myself to believe that it would be so. But I suppose it is necessary once in a while to prove that there is something else in the world to attend to than the behests of fair ladies.

JOSEPH: Oh, my dearest Carrie—

CARRIE: Now, just see how good I am. I not only forgive you for your shortcomings yesterday, but I ask you to come out here tomorrow afternoon.

JOSEPH: Tomorrow afternoon....

CARRIE: I don't know why—it's just a little weakness of mine which of course you are bound to regard with charity—but I want to see you. And you know you *are* going away Tuesday. To think when in my first note yesterday I made so touching a little reference to the fact of your soon going away, and in the next asked you in so many words to come out, you didn't take the least notice of either!

JOSEPH: My dearest Carrie—

CARRIE: I've been looking over the only two notes you've written me since last Sunday; and do you know, in all there are not more than a dozen lines!

JOSEPH: Carrie—

CARRIE: *Mon bien aimé,* I *have* missed your letters this week.

JOSEPH: Carrie, dearest—

CARRIE: Well, come out tomorrow if you can, and I will not reproach you. Mother says you must stay all night if you come. And you and I will take that pretty wood walk of ours on Monday morning.

JOSEPH: When I come tomorrow I will bring you one of my long articles, that I may prove to you that stern duty and not pleasure has kept me from the company of my own dear heart.

CARRIE: If Father hands this note to you, I give you permission to tear a scrap from my sheet and *write* a word of message.

JOSEPH: Write?

CARRIE: Somehow for some absurd reason I feel uncomfortably *conscious* when Father brings me a verbal message.

JOSEPH (*smiling*): My dearest Carrie!

CARRIE: You'll begin to think I'm full of what you call "whims," won't you? Never mind: you're bound to put up with them now.

JOSEPH: Dearest Carrie, when I see you next you must be *very, very good* to me.

CARRIE (*smiling*): Very, very good?

JOSEPH: You know, I shall not see you again for some time.

CARRIE: Darling Joe, shall I say how long it has seemed since last Sunday night? And how I look forward to tomorrow afternoon? And how I *do not* look forward to the four months that are to follow? No, I won't say anything of the kind: it just makes you arrogant and conceited. Ah, but I can't help saying it. There—I won't say another word.... Here are some vastly sentimental lines that I am almost ashamed to send. But they are so pretty. Of course I only send them for their poetical merit. They are Mrs. Browning's. (*She reads.*)

> Go from me. Yet I feel that I shall stand
> Henceforward in thy shadow. Nevermore
> Alone upon the threshold of my door
> Of individual life, I shall command
> The uses of my soul, nor lift my hand
> Serenely in the sunshine as before.
> ....
> ....The widest land
> Doom takes to part us, leaves thy heart in mine
> With pulses that beat double. What I do
> And what I dream include thee, as the wine
> Must taste of its own grapes. And when I sue
> God for myself, He hears that name of thine,
> And sees within my eyes the tears of two.

What shall I say unto my beloved than that he is always with me—that his love rejoices me every hour of the day, and at night "I sleep, but my heart waketh, for I hear the voice of my beloved."

JOSEPH: Is not this a splendid night? Have you enjoyed these moonlight nights? If I were only with you, my darling—you whose fairness surpasses that of the moon! (My love, you *are* fairer than the moon.)

CARRIE: Are you at this moment sitting in that cozy library with the firelight playing upon your books, and your thoughts playing in several directions at once?

JOSEPH: You are with me, darling, around the cheerful fire. And my heart beats close to yours, and my arms encircle you, and my lips are giving you the longest and tenderest kisses.

CARRIE: Shall I lay my head on your bosom, and clasp my

hands around your waist as you love to have me do? And shall I sit beside you for the rest of the evening?

JOSEPH: Again and again, my own dear Carrie, when the tedious labors of the day are over, I sit and think of you—recall our delightful moonlight walks, treasure your lovely image, and dwell upon your looks of the deepest, truest love.

CARRIE: This evening, my own dear Joe, I shall spend a long, long time with you.

JOSEPH: Do you often think of our walk in the woods that warm May morning?

CARRIE (*smiling*): I remember it was *your* fault that my hair came down.

JOSEPH: Do you know, the image of your flowing tresses in the sunlight has inexpressible charms for me.

CARRIE (*smiling*): I never mean to take a walk with you again.

JOSEPH: And now I will step into the garden and pluck you the sweetest flowers that I can find.

CARRIE: Good angels guard you! Pleasant thoughts be your companions! And every good gift be showered upon you, my best beloved!

JOSEPH: It is now the still hour of midnight. I put my arms around you and take you in my sweetest embrace, and give you ten thousand of the warmest seals of love, and lay my head upon my dear, sweet, pure, true, lovely, precious home, and recall every precious word and every sweet look, and listen to that sweet voice (the sweetest and softest that ever moved my heart), and pass imperceptibly into the land of dreams.

CARRIE: One long, tender kiss, my dearest Joe. Do you feel it on your lips? Do you feel my arms around your waist? Do you feel my heart close to yours? Good night, my best beloved, my own, my life. Am I not yours now and forever? Take from me my love, my heart, everything that you will have....

FADEOUT

Act Two

As the stage lights come up, Joseph Jones *is seated at a desk, writing.*

Joseph: This is my first Sabbath at Maybank, and here I am at its close, holding sweet communion with you, my own dear love. The glorious sun is just sinking behind the distant trees; his soft rays light up the intervening verdant fields, upon which the cattle are quietly grazing, and then fall into my little room. I am sitting at the window, overlooking an extensive green marsh, now overflowed with the high summer tide, and the rays of the setting sun gild each wave and ripple. All nature is beautiful. But with me one thing is wanting: the light and joy of my life is absent. Oh, that you, my own, were with me at this calm hour!

Carrie: *Amigo mio. Mein Geliebt. Ami de mon âme.* I would like, my dearest Joe, to call in several other languages and see if I could find some term by which I might begin this my first letter since you left me; but they will not any of them express anything I want to express. So suppose for this once I lay aside my fears of spoiling you and call you in "our own dear mother tongue" what my heart prompts and my pen writes almost without my will: "My own beloved." It is only five days since you left me, but it seems a long time; and I was rejoiced to get your letter from Savannah yesterday morning.

Joseph: I was very anxious about you on Tuesday.

Carrie: I was not afraid of the horses, but I *would* have been glad if you could have driven back with us.... That was a scanty leave-taking there on Broad Street, but I hardly dared look at you for fear of profane eyes; so that cool shake of the hand was all.

JOSEPH: I met Dr. Campbell at the railroad station, and we came on to Savannah together.

CARRIE: Did you know, *mon bien aimé*, why I took such an unimpressive leave of you? I felt very sad, and would fain have cried right out; but there was such constant passing I did not wish anyone else to have the benefit of a scene. And so, beloved, I let you go thinking that this separation of four months is nothing. It *is*, though, you will believe me.

JOSEPH: I reached the Island on Wednesday afternoon after a hot ride, and found Mother quite well and Father in his usual health.

CARRIE: All day I have been thinking of you at home. Were they glad to see you? And are you not very happy in being there?

JOSEPH: We have had a bright, beautiful day. I have never seen the atmosphere more transparent, or the trees and fields dressed in richer green.... This morning as I sat in the piazza all nature seemed to be rejoicing. The mockingbirds were singing in every grove and tree. The squirrels were playing in our flower garden only a few steps from the house, and eating their morning repast of corn, and quarreling with our pet cat. Two little orchard orioles were feeding their young on a swinging limb only a few yards from the roof of the house; the lover was very kind to his ladylove, and would not only catch insects and butterflies and bring them to the clamorous little family but also enliven the toils of his fair one with a merry song.

CARRIE: It must be a life of great charm. What a splendid place it will be for my professor to work out his philosophic problems and dream his philosophic dreams!

JOSEPH: I am busily at work on my article.

CARRIE: But he mustn't let either his philosophy or his dreams withdraw him too much from actual life. I should grow jealous if they did.

JOSEPH: After breakfast I read in an old book written by Thomas à Kempis: *The Christian Pattern; or, A Treatise on the Imitation of Jesus Christ*. Father had service for the servants. There was no preaching within twenty miles, so we all remained at home. After dinner I conducted Mother's Sabbath school for the servants.

CARRIE: Dear Joe, how I should like to have even one glimpse of you! How much more should I like to have you here, that we might spend Sunday together as we several times have!

JOSEPH: The bell for supper is ringing, and I must lay my pen aside.

CARRIE: You and I do not "forget the Sabbath Day to keep it holy" when we write to each other, do you think? I always feel that to hold communion with the spirit of him whom my soul loveth is most specially befitting the day.

JOSEPH: It is now ten o'clock, and here I am again alone with my pen. After supper Mother, Father, Sister, and I revived an old custom which is connected with the memories of my earliest childhood. We sat in the piazza, enjoying the cool sea breeze, and conversing on solemn subjects, and singing all the old hymns which I had learned with Sister and Brother in childhood. After family prayers I read aloud in Bunyan's *Pilgrim's Progress*. My cup of happiness would have been full if you, my precious, could have formed one of this dear circle.

CARRIE: Will you not remember me very specially to your father and mother and Mary?

JOSEPH: Would that I had the power to annihilate the time and distance which now separate our hearts! Although I am surrounded by the dearest relatives and friends, I feel lonely; and my heart dwells not in their home, not even in the home of my childhood, but ever in the dear, dear home which you, my dearest love, have given me.... Yesterday I looked anxiously for a letter from you. There was one which in its envelope and direction resembled your letters. Without a moment's delay I tore off the seal; to my surprise and chagrin the letter was not from you and not even for me; it belonged to Sister. I had to confess to her that I had read the direction with the eyes of love, which are said to be blind. When I sat down and calmly counted the days of our separation, I found that I had no right to expect a letter from you until the next mail.

CARRIE: Do you remember, I once told you that your letters reminded me of what was said of Foster's *Essays:* "the grandest love letters that were ever written." If I should express a hundredth part of what I feel in reading them, my beloved, I am afraid you would think I went too far and would ask me to recur to that *cool* and *distant* style I once practiced and threaten to adopt again. This one time, though, I must write as I feel. I must tell you how when I read them I feel that I could give up house and home and friends and follow to the ends of the earth the man who writes such words of love. Are you shocked that I should write so much? I never could if you were not at a distance. Ah, I am breaking through all my rules—saying a good many things that perhaps I shall feel sorry for.

JOSEPH: My darling, how shall I thank you—how *can* I thank you—for your many expressions of love?

CARRIE: You must not dismiss my expressions of love as fond folly.

JOSEPH: My dearest Carrie, they are my life, my joy, my rest, my peace!

CARRIE: If you had rather I would not write them, I never will again.

JOSEPH: Darling, you know I value them above diamonds—above the wealth of California!

CARRIE: Does it make you happy to think that I love you? If it does, I will tell you, as I have never told you before, how with a love that is almost anguish my heart goes out to yours.

JOSEPH: Near the close of dinner the mail arrived. Some of our friends were taking a social dinner with us; I was sitting at the front of the table, and was doing the honors of the occasion. My eyes had been directed to the door, anxiously waiting the appearance of the messenger; and by a significant nod I conveyed my command to bring me the mail first without attracting the attention of the company. As soon as my eye rested upon your dear familiar hand, all interest in passing conversation vanished; and in a few moments I attempted to disband the company by remarking to my old Uncle William Maxwell that he must be tired sitting so long, and that he must not confine himself to the table; and with this I gave a slight push, and the strategem succeeded. As soon as they rose, I hastened to my room and devoured your precious letter.

CARRIE: And so you have had only one letter from me since you left. That letter I am glad you received, for there are many things in it I shall probably never say again.

JOSEPH: I have thought a thousand times of the *sweet* moments, the *precious* moments, the *sacred* moments that I spent with my dearest Carrie that last Sabbath in Augusta.

CARRIE: Did you enjoy your Sabbath with me?

JOSEPH: It was the happiest Sabbath I ever spent.

CARRIE: Every moment of the day was precious to me.

JOSEPH: Did you know that I had never said those Psalms to anyone in this world before except to my dear mother?

CARRIE: I knew that you had never said those Psalms to anyone else but your mother, and it seemed to bring me into a nearer relation to you.

JOSEPH: If I am anything I owe it all to the prayers and pious instructions and generous liberality of my dear parents, and to the gentle influence of a kind sister, and to your own ennobling influence, my guardian angel—my spirit of light and love and truth.

CARRIE: Do you know, I have often had a sort of dream of such a Sunday. A waking dream: a Sunday when I should hold your dear head and feel that the touch of my hand was cool and soothing. Ah, I do not believe there is on earth one feeling so near akin to heaven as the bliss of ministering to those we love.

JOSEPH: You see, my own dear precious Carrie, that I am making amends for that unkind lecture I gave you the evening we parted.

CARRIE: Lecture?

JOSEPH: I have long since repented of it, and you have long since heaped coals of *love,* not fire—yes, the fire of love—upon my willing head.

CARRIE: You speak of the conversation we had in the woods.

JOSEPH: I never told you why I was grieved by your remarks. You remember, darling, that you told me in the woods that "were it not for the conventionalities of society you would prefer remaining simply as a friend; that you did not see the use of marriage aside from the conventionalities of society." Dearest, have I quoted your words correctly?

CARRIE: You have.

JOSEPH: Those words stunned me as if I had suddenly struck my head against a stone wall. I had given you everything; my heart had been laid at your feet. And after all this were you never to be more to me than a friend?... But it has all passed. You have told me that you do love me as I love you—*love for love*. My own dear Carrie, will you not forgive me for misunderstanding you?

CARRIE: I think I mentioned that Shakespeare is a favorite authority of mine. I quote some lines of his which you may either look upon in the light of their literary merit or else apply as you think proper. (*She recites.*)

> His words are bonds, his oaths are oracles,
> His love sincere, his thoughts immaculate,
> His tears pure messengers sent from his heart,
> His heart as far from fraud as heaven from earth.

Don't you think that's a noble description? To find someone who would come up to that *used* to be quite "my sigh after the infinite," as they say in German.... Dearest Joe, if my words sound stiff and cool, do not think that *I* am stiff and cool. Do you know, at this moment I should like to be sitting beside you with my hand on that dear head, and that dearer heart beating only a little way off. Sometimes, do you know, when I haven't seen you for two or three days, I feel famished for one long, tender kiss. You will not now think me stiff and cool?

JOSEPH: My dearest Carrie, I cannot write poetry; but if I could all my powers would be employed in celebrating *our love*. When I attempt to tell you how much I love you, words seem but noisy breath. (*He reads.*)

> To Carrie
> She walks in beauty, like the night
> > Of cloudless climes and starry skies;
> And all that's best of dark and bright
> > Meet in her aspect and her eyes:
> Thus mellow'd to that tender light
> > Which heaven to gaudy day denies.
>
> One shade the more, one ray the less,
> > Had half impair'd the nameless grace
> Which waves in every golden* tress,
> > Or softly lightens o'er her face;
> Where thoughts serenely sweet express
> > How pure, how dear their dwelling place.
>
> And on that cheek, and o'er that brow,
> > So soft, so calm, yet eloquent,
> The smiles that win, the tints that glow,
> > But tell of days in goodness spent,
> A mind at peace with all below,
> > A heart whose love is innocent!

Do you remember, Carrie, what you told me as we parted that last evening?

CARRIE: I told you I did not know what I had ever done for you or could do for you.

JOSEPH: Is your pure, warm love nothing? Is love which will outlast the changes of time nothing?

CARRIE: Did you ever notice how *hurried* our good-byes always seem to be? And how *public*? Shall I tell you—just in a whisper, now, in your ear—shall I tell you how I wanted to go out to the door with you that evening, but reflected that all the doors and windows were wide open, and so did not venture?

---

*Byron's text reads *raven;* the actor playing JOSEPH should render the word *golden* with some slight indication (a hint of hesitation? a shift in emphasis or tone?) that the substitution is deliberate.

JOSEPH: Do you know, I lingered not only on the steps but also in the garden. I thought I heard the footsteps of my dearest, and my heart leaped within my bosom.

CARRIE: I heard you linger down the steps, and by the time you fairly reached the buggy I got up my courage and went to the door, but you were gone.

JOSEPH: I walked back several steps, but I could see no one. Perhaps the tree hid you from my view.

CARRIE: So it is, *mon cher,* there are things in the world we are just one moment too late for.

JOSEPH: Never mind, my angel: I will take the will for the deed till we meet again.

CARRIE (*smiling*): Ah....

JOSEPH: If you knew what exquisite delight those tokens of your love afford, you would sometimes spoil your own Joseph.

CARRIE (*smiling*): Ah....

JOSEPH: Here I am at the still hour of midnight communing with your dear spirit after the tedious labors of the day. As I write, a delightful mockingbird is cheering his sweetheart and her little family with his merry song. They have their nest of young ones just by the window where I write and study.... Do you know, I have devoted my short evenings sacredly to you. As I walk by the silent banks of the river, and view the setting sun as it gilds the sluggish waters winding through the broad marshes, every beautiful cloud, every luxuriant tree, every note of a seabird brings a fervent wish that you, my dearest love, were with me.... This evening I looked up the road until my eyes ached, longing for the mailbag, and finally I had to go over to Social Bluff without hearing from you. When I returned at ten o'clock, I rushed into the house thinking: "Surely the postboy has arrived with a letter from Carrie!" But, alas, there was not a line from my sweetheart!

CARRIE: *Were* you disappointed at not hearing from me? It was not my fault. I had my letter all ready, but long before dark the rain poured as if the windows of heaven were indeed opened, and so it could not go down that night.

JOSEPH: Your dear letter has this day arrived, and I am sorry—nay, grieved—that my letters have not reached you. I have written you almost every mail. We have now only two mails during the week, and I live fifteen miles from the post office. Just to think, to get your letters or to send my letters I or the servant must ride *thirty miles*—and this, too, in summer! So you will not consider me an unworthy lover if you do not receive a letter four or five times a week.... As I cannot send you flowers, every morning I pick the sweetest roses and lay them amongst my paper and envelopes with the hope that I can send you at least a hint of their fragrance.

CARRIE: Dear Joe, I was delighted to receive the *fan*.

JOSEPH: I will try, my love, and kill a pink spoonbill or a white crane and secure the feathers for a *bridal* fan.

CARRIE: How are you today? Is it as cool and autumnal down there as it is up here? *We* are in great beauty now: the grass as fresh as early springtime, our cypress tent in great perfection, and a crepe myrtle in the most radiant bloom down at the circular bed. It is a pleasure just to sit and look out.

JOSEPH: I have not as yet heard from Philadelphia. I hope my article has gone safely, and is now in the hands of the printer. I feel quite anxious for my six-hundred-page manuscript. Would it not be unfortunate if it were lost!

CARRIE: I was going to tell you what I had been doing today, but upon mature reflection there is nothing to tell. I must have gone through that usual noiseless routine of woman's work. And then I read ever so much to Father, spelling Julia, who had read ever so much before. Then I walked to the tollgate and came back tired to death, which will perhaps account for the peculiar brilliancy of this note.

JOSEPH: My dear Carrie, I send you two daguerreotypes—one of Mother and one of Sister.

CARRIE (*delighted*): Oh, Joe!

JOSEPH: Is not that of Mother (the small one) a fine specimen of the art?

CARRIE: I can scarcely decide when I saw her for so short a time. But how admirable Mary's is!

JOSEPH: You see that Sister's is not exactly a full-face.

CARRIE: I never saw a more agreeable likeness.

JOSEPH: Suppose, my love, that you try a similar position.

CARRIE: A similar position....

JOSEPH: And I hope you will display as much of your figure as possible.

CARRIE: Ah....

JOSEPH: In fact, *all* would suit me best.

CARRIE: But, dearest Joe—

JOSEPH: One great objection to the likeness I have is that it doesn't display your elegant figure.

CARRIE: My dearest Joe—

JOSEPH: And you must not hide your neck in lace.

CARRIE: Dearest Joe, touching the personal appearance of the elect lady—

JOSEPH: Yes?

CARRIE: Ah, Joe, sometimes she looks very plain indeed—pale sometimes, and very thin.

JOSEPH: Pale and thin? Have you been sick? My precious Carrie, you must tell me all!

CARRIE: Do not let your eyes too fondly look forward to resting upon a beauty which has, I fear, never been anywhere but in your eyes.

JOSEPH: Do you know, my darling, I keep your dear image always by my side when I am writing or reading or studying.

CARRIE: This morning as soon as the weather permitted, "correspondent to command" I went down to have my fugitive traits detained for your benefit, and I hope I have succeeded better than before.

JOSEPH: I am happy to inform you, my love, that I have received a letter from Professor Francis Gurney Smith of Philadelphia stating that my article has been received and is now in the hands of the printer.

CARRIE: I congratulate you upon hearing of your manuscript. I have been greatly concerned at its long delay.

JOSEPH: And now, my precious Carrie, I will soon be with you.

CARRIE (*overjoyed*): My dearest Joe!

JOSEPH: If Providence permits, I hope to leave for Augusta on the 22nd or 23rd of this month. I must remain in Savannah one day on account of the shipment of my books and household matters from the Albany & Gulf Railroad to the Savannah & Augusta Railroad. I hope to be with you at all events on Saturday the 24th of September.

CARRIE: It is hardly necessary for me to say, dear Joe, that you must not let anything I say hasten your movements. You know I always want to see you, but if your attendance on your father or your own engagements of any kind make it desirable, you should stay in the low country as long as you can. Poor Joe, it is your last free time; you must by all means enjoy it while you may.

JOSEPH: Oh, Carrie, will we not be happy when we meet!

CARRIE: Oh, Joe!

JOSEPH: I know you are going to be very good to me.

CARRIE (*smiling*): Ah....

JOSEPH: For you have made me many sweet promises.

CARRIE (*smiling*): Ah....

JOSEPH: I will claim them all with compound interest.

CARRIE: Oh, Joe!

JOSEPH: And I will return them all a thousand times multiplied.

CARRIE: I know, my dearest Don José, that you will wish to find a welcoming note; so behold me like a devoted fiancée seated with my new paper and new pen, bending my efforts to that effect.

JOSEPH: Tell me, love, when you would prefer me to come and see you—in the morning or in the evening?

CARRIE: If you should arrive tomorrow morning, as I hope and expect, don't come out until the afternoon. You will be dreadfully tired, and will need some rest. But send me word that you have returned and are well; that is all I shall want until I see you in the afternoon.

JOSEPH: The time that you prefer will suit me best.

CARRIE: Now, dear Joe, don't *think* of coming out here in the morning. I shall not even *want* to see you; and you *must rest* after being up all night. Only send me word.... Ah, *mon cher,* these lovely, lovely autumn days I have thought of you often and wished you could have spent them out here. Do you know, autumn is my favorite season. And this is the first autumn of our acquaintance. I think nothing in the world so appeals to one's fancy as these long, bright, purple autumn days. It has always been my dream to associate with autumn the great happiness of my life. And my dream has been fulfilled.

JOSEPH: Before I forget it—I have made out the wedding list and will bring it when I come.

CARRIE: Perhaps I shall want to see you in two or three days about the address of some of those invitations.

JOSEPH: Darling, the arrangements shall be exactly as best suits your taste. We will not invite the faculty, and we will have the marriage in your own home.

CARRIE: Dearest Joe, out of consideration for my family I should like—indeed I *must* leave home a few hours after the ceremony. I know it will be an immense convenience to Mother to have me out of the way for a few days. I shall not care what you decide so long as you consider this little whim of mine.

JOSEPH: My dearest love, your reasons for preferring the trip to Clarkesville are just, and it shall be as you wish.

CARRIE: Clarkesville....

JOSEPH: My chief desire is to carry out your wishes with reference to quiet and seclusion.

CARRIE: But, dearest, what has become of you? What is the matter with you? Are you sick or sad or mad? All afternoon I watched for your buggy, thinking surely you would be up; and now it is ever so much o'clock. Every possibility of hearing from you has gone; and I have resorted as usual in such an extreme case to several cups of tea, which threaten to hold my eyes waking for ever so long; so I employ my wakefulness in writing to ask you what has happened to prevent either your coming or sending out some message.... I am afraid you are sick. That was a shocking storm you went down in last night, and you had a headache then. Ah, how many unseasonable drives I have made you take!

JOSEPH: But, dearest Carrie, I enjoyed my visit.

CARRIE: Even though your head did ache?

JOSEPH: Ah, but you cured it.

CARRIE: 'Twas a pleasant way of curing it.

JOSEPH: 'Twas a pleasant way indeed.

CARRIE: I should like to have the same power of charming away all care and pain from the head and heart of my own.

JOSEPH: I am much better today.

CARRIE: I hope you will be well enough to come out tomorrow.

JOSEPH: My beloved, on account of my head it will be best for me to remain quiet for two or three days.

CARRIE: Consider my hands laid upon your head and the pain all willed away. There—is it gone?

JOSEPH: If I do not come tomorrow, remember that your bright image is always with me.

CARRIE: By the way, darling, speaking of your head: I have concluded that I will have you go to the barber and have your hair cut and arranged after the very last turn of fashion. It must be long enough to come below your ears; it must be parted just as much and no more to the side than the fashion requires; and your "back hair" must be arranged with the strictest regard to the mode.... I do sigh over those lovelocks; I can't help it. The only reparation I make myself is to have you bring me some of the longest pieces.... Don't you think my tea has affected my brain?... There, now—they have come for my note. Don't you call this a freewill offering?

JOSEPH: Many, many thanks, my dear Carrie, for the "freewill offering." I have read it again and again and pressed it to my heart.

CARRIE: Father tells me you were out this morning, apparently quite well. Ah, I know better than that. I know that apology for a "trembling hand" meant you had been sick, and those two short pages (I will not tell you how delightful they were to me) meant you were not well enough to write more.

JOSEPH: The reason that my hand trembled was that I had been writing rapidly all day and my fingers were weary.

CARRIE: Darling Joe, you *must not* study too much. This physician, if he cannot heal himself, at least must not break all the laws of the healing art.... And now, do you know, I am going to give you a real lecture. I believe you think that all my talk about the duty of taking care of your health has been merely at random; but indeed it has not. I am in the most serious earnest: you work too hard; you expose yourself too much; you drive out to see me when you ought to be lying down.... And now you are anxious about that address you are preparing. I should like to make you promise that until you have finished that address you will go back to the free, unfettered state of mind in which you rejoiced nine months ago.... I do so want you to satisfy yourself in your present work. I know others will be more than satisfied, and I quite look forward to the applause that will follow your effort; but I know you will not care for that unless *you* are satisfied.... Do you think if you were not to come out here for a week it would aid you? Because if it would, in that spirit of self-abnegation which is considered one of the principal virtues of the weak sisterhood, I deny myself and tell you that that will please me most.

JOSEPH: Carrie darling, I cannot take your advice about visiting. I must see you as often as possible.

CARRIE: Don't you mean to take my advice? Will you not believe how much *my* happiness is concerned?

JOSEPH: Just to think, you take such interest in my health and welfare!

CARRIE: I am very sorry that in return for a letter which made me *so happy* I should have sent you in not even a card; but I could only have accomplished a note by being late to prayers and breakfast. I am sure, dear Joe, if you were ever guilty of any such breach of family etiquette when you dwelt under the parental roof you know the kind of reproachful salutation that greets such conduct. So I forbore, having a secret hope that you might be tempted out this afternoon. But the latest minute that I ever expect you has passed and you are not here, so I seat myself to write my second note today.

JOSEPH: Second?

CARRIE: Don't be alarmed and think that some unfaithful slave has dropped the first in the canal or lost it in the mud between here and your house. I wrote it at the rate of ten knots an hour after breakfast; but Father and Mother, unaware of how I was engaged, *would* start into town before it was finished; and so that was the way you lost it. Upon a reperusal it didn't suit me without so many revisions that it was better to begin afresh.... Just to think how this day on which I *might* have seen you has been wasted!... This morning I rearranged your flowers. I quite exhausted my genius in arranging the various vases about, and you don't know how this wilderness is beginning to blossom like a rose.... Then I walked down to Milledge's spring, and it was so lovely I wished a hundred times you had been with me. The air and woods and sky were splendid beyond description. I passed that spot on the hillside where you and I sat one bright spring morning, and I remembered the deadly designs you had against a poor innocent little boy who unwittingly passed because you said: "Dead men tell no tales."... I have been lying down all afternoon—not sick at all, but just so comfortably indisposed as to ease my conscience.... What have *you* been doing all this time? Have you wanted to come out? Just to think, I have not for one moment doubted that you had rather be walking or talking or sitting with me than reading the most delightful scientific work on the loveliest case of the rarest disease ever known!

JOSEPH: How I wish that I could have been with you, my own, this bright, beautiful day!

CARRIE: Poor Joe, how many pages of proof have you been wearying over while I have been enjoying the sunshine with no more laborious subject of thought than just yourself!

JOSEPH: You, my dearest, have been with me all day during my labors in correcting proofs.

CARRIE: I was not wrong, I find, in picturing you over your proofs.

JOSEPH: You know I told you I had received my new bookcases, and I have just been arranging my books.

CARRIE: Dear, dear Joe, how I wish I could help you!

JOSEPH: I have not been idle one second since I left you.

CARRIE: I wonder what you are doing at this moment.

JOSEPH: I am trying to write my address, but it moves forward slowly.

CARRIE: I am sitting at my window writing too, but a different sort of address from yours, and feeling very much inclined to give hard names to certain people who have called and so interrupted me I have to go. Write to me often, my own: your letters are my life.

JOSEPH: My darling, one of your letters is worth a dozen of mine.

CARRIE: You excused my not answering your note last night, didn't you? I had not the heart to detain the bishop of Crete from "meeting"; it would have seemed really cruel.

JOSEPH: This is the Sabbath evening. I have not been with you this day, but I have thought of you a thousand times. What have you been doing?

CARRIE: I was at church this morning, and heard some queer quotations from Milton. I was not edified.

JOSEPH: Milton....

CARRIE: Tonight if you are out you will hear a sermon on Samson, and I presume you will hear quotations from the *Agonistes*. The next time you see me tell me if there is not a picturesque description of Delilah in the course of the sermon.... Oh, I ought to be ashamed, oughtn't I? But *what* I would give to hear strong preaching!

JOSEPH: This morning I was much gratified with the interest manifested in the Sabbath school. There were more than a hundred attendants. In the singing I was greatly assisted by the colored choir, who conducted the singing with melody and spirit. The Africans are very fond of music.

CARRIE: I looked round as I came out of church to see if peradventure you might have strayed up, but I saw you not.... When your note came, I was just in the midst of reading one of Dr. Spurgeon's sermons aloud to Father, and I expect you to applaud my forbearance and give me ten kisses for the self-denial I practiced in reading to the very end before I broke the seal.

JOSEPH: Was it wrong for me to commune with the heart I love on the Sabbath Day?

CARRIE: If it was wrong, it was a wrong I shared. My thoughts wandered dreadfully in church; and in the afternoon those luminous arguments of Dr. Spurgeon got inextricably wound up with foolish, fond reasonings of my own.

JOSEPH: Then you will not blame me if your image was before me all day?

CARRIE: And to think *I* meant to ask *you* if *you* thought it wrong! How foolish of me to make any such unnecessary admission! Yes, it was a great mistake. I am painfully conscious of how much I have lost in your opinion as a firm, cool, calculating woman.... Yes, I was thinking of you all day, wondering all manner of things about you—if you were engaged in good works abroad or meditating at home; if you were reading or writing or thinking; if you were lonely.... I can picture you now in your library, sitting in the firelight, dreaming of a companionship not merely of books. Do you want me with you? I think I should give anything to see you just for a moment in the Sunday twilight.... But, my dearest Joe, you forgot entirely to tell me whether you went to church and heard about Delilah!

JOSEPH: Dr. Wilson gave us a very good sermon this evening. I thought of you.... Four little orphans sat just opposite me. The poor little fellows went to sleep and snored vigorously. My heart was full when I thought that they had no kind mother to care for all their little wants.... Should not you and I be very thankful that we have such pious parents?

CARRIE: I drove into town this morning, and was thinking how often I am in and how seldom I see you. I have never glimpsed you in the street since that day long ago when you wouldn't look at me. Do you remember?

JOSEPH (*smiling*): I do not remember.

CARRIE: I longed to catch a glimpse of you this morning; but the nearest I came to it was to see a most formidable packet addressed to Professor Jones which I fear was another detachment of those dreadful proofs. I saw every member of the medical faculty but just the only one I wanted to see. Isn't that always the way? There they all were; but you, I suppose, were deep in your address, or busy at the museum sticking pins in your subjects, or looking complacently round at the various domestic arrangements you express such a desire I should get a glimpse of, and which, to tell the truth, I should like to see myself.

JOSEPH: For a novelty I went to market this morning and bought some chickens and ducks.

CARRIE (*amused*): Chickens and ducks!

JOSEPH: Several of the lady chickens are to be permanent inhabitants of our yard—provided that their residence meets with the approbation of their mistress.

CARRIE: While you are busily engaged in your profound reflections I am frivolously engaged with my dressmaker—the results of which occupation will gradually develop themselves to your unaccustomed eyes in the course of the next few weeks, and will, I don't doubt, astonish you. For instance: who can calculate the effect of a certain little rose-colored arrangement which will dawn upon you first in—Clarkesville.

JOSEPH: Clarkesville....

CARRIE: Perhaps one of these days when I turn in to arranging your books, and seriously aspire to correcting your proofs, and propose myself as the translator of French articles (always leaving out the technical parts), and make myself in a humble way generally useful to my lord, I shall feel a greater degree of complacency in myself than I do at present. Now my ambition is bounded by the longing to hold the tired head of my beloved when it aches with too much thought, and to feel his arm around my waist sustaining *me*.

JOSEPH: I am glad, my dearest, that you have decided upon a

personal attendant. I had determined to hire one for you; but this arrangement will be much better than any I could make, as you know this servant personally.

CARRIE: It is difficult to obtain honest and intelligent hired servants unless you know them personally.

JOSEPH: I will endeavor to render my cook as accomplished as possible. Did I ever tell you that my man Titus can also cook very well?

CARRIE: This will be convenient in case of sickness.

JOSEPH: I think you will find both of your servants, Titus and Phillis (our cook), obedient and good-natured domestics, and withal very honest.

CARRIE: Honesty is a most valuable trait in servants.

JOSEPH: Will you not tell me every arrangement you wish me to make?

CARRIE: Darling Joe, I do want to see you dreadfully. I can hardly believe it was only yesterday you were up here. If your business admits of it, come out tomorrow and dine.

JOSEPH: My darling, you must tell me truly if I am interrupting your duties or interfering with your arrangements or violating any established custom.

CARRIE: And if you can spare the time to dine, you can give me that charming drive in the afternoon.

JOSEPH: I will be with you tomorrow, and we will ride out.

CARRIE: Besides, I have had a box today from New York.

JOSEPH: A box....

CARRIE: Containing that veil of which I have spoken.

JOSEPH: Ah....

CARRIE: And tomorrow I want to try it on. So if you are here you just may be included in the privilege of seeing me in it.

JOSEPH: Ah....

CARRIE: And what do you think of Mrs. S. S. Davis's having the complaisance to be "at home" to Professor Joseph Jones, M. D., next Wednesday evening the 26th of October?

JOSEPH: Ah....

CARRIE: Do you think you will accept? If you decide otherwise, send in your regrets early. You know, that is quite an important point of etiquette.

JOSEPH: Ah. . . .

CARRIE: Well, the cards are all issued now: your doom is fixed. Do you repent? Do you think you've been rash?

JOSEPH: Dearest Carrie—

CARRIE: By the way, I have had two lovely presents today—one from my friends Mary and Retta Carmichael: an elegant silver butter stand; and the other from Sister: a beautiful set of tea china. She brought me out a cup as a specimen which I will show you when you come; the rest is to remain packed until I come *home.*

JOSEPH (*smiling*): Home. . . .

CARRIE: I have taken this *tiny* sheet of paper because I have just a *tiny* moment to write previous to starting out again to complete a perfect campaign of visiting in which I have been engaged all day: P. P. C. calls—"taking leave" calls—which have been hanging over me for several weeks—the last I will make as "Miss Caroline Davis." Don't you think I ought to feel just one little emotion as I draw so near the end of my claim on my old name?

JOSEPH: My dearest, it is growing late; and as Titus has to return this evening, I will have to allow him some time to rest on The Hill and "go to meeting."

CARRIE: This note—which perhaps I should not be writing—is just filling up a little space until Father shall be ready to hear me read. . . . I thought of you, dearest, a great deal yesterday. As I put the last stitches to that lovely morning robe we displayed to you Friday evening, I wandered off for a moment to Clarkesville and the first morning when I shall array myself in it. . . . As I read that address, though, I made up for the frivolity of that last thought by indulging in a certain naughty perhaps but very delightful pride in the name and fame of my own beloved. The writing I think fine, and the thought finer. And do not think I just say so. . . . This morning as I sat in church it came over me that it was the last Sunday I should ever again be in that pew with my own name. I thought to myself: "When I am no longer alone, shall I be another person?" ... I have been reading and thinking and thinking and reading all day; and in an old volume of Jeremy Taylor I found "A Prayer to be Said by a Maiden Before She Enter the State of Marriage." (*She reads.*)

"Lord, bless and preserve that dear person whom thou hast chosen to be my husband. Let this life be long and blessed, comfortable and holy, and let me also become a great blessing and comfort unto him—a sharer in all his joys, a refreshment in all his sorrows, a meet helper for him in all accidents and chances of the world. Make me amiable forever in his eyes, and very dear to him. Unite his heart to me in the dearest union of love and holiness, and mine to him in all sweetness and charity and compliance. Keep from me all morosity and ungentleness, all sullenness and harshness of disposition, all pride and vanity, all discontentedness and unreasonableness of passion and humor; and make me humble and obedient, charitable and loving, patient and contented, useful and observant—that both of us may rejoice in Thee, having our portion in the love and service of God forever and ever."

Dear Joe, I fear I am very far from being capable of all that; but with God's help and with your love to sustain me I shall *try*. Isn't it a beautiful prayer!

JOSEPH: I have prayed that beautiful prayer, my darling. I feel assured that God will answer it, and bless you with peace and light and love and joy.

CARRIE: *Mon bien aimé,* I fear I shall not make you a good wife.

JOSEPH: My own Carrie, you *will* make me a good wife—the best wife, the prettiest, the sweetest, the dearest, the happiest, the fondest wife in this wide, wide world.

CARRIE: I shall be everything to you that a wife can be to a beloved husband.

JOSEPH: Will not the long winter evenings be pleasant when we will sit around our own hearth and read and converse?

CARRIE: Well, they are calling to me vociferously from downstairs. I have told Titus to come back for this note after going to meeting;

but as I *must* return to the circle in the parlor, I shall have to stop now.... I cannot tell when you may come out again, but I incline to seeing you on Tuesday morning if you can spare a little time. Wednesday, of course, you *could* not come; and I *should* like to see you once more.

JOSEPH: My dear Carrie, how are you this bright, pleasant morning? Do you not see that all nature is smiling upon our union? Are you not happy?... Mother and Father and Sister and Brother Robert and Brother Charles arrived safely last evening; and this morning Aunt Susan and Cousin Lyman Buttolph joined our happy circle.... In a few moments Mother wishes me to go out with her to one of the stores on Main Street; and Father wishes me to go with him to Dr. Wilson's; and I have to see about my household affairs and dinner; and I am sure, my sweetheart, my darling, my own most precious Carrie, that you will forgive the forlorn appearance of this note, which has been scribbled in the midst of conversation. God bless you, my own!

CARRIE: Dearest Joe—

JOSEPH: By Titus, the bishop of Crete, we send you some little mementos from our relatives and friends.

CARRIE: Ah, Joe, everybody is a great deal too good to us! What do you think we have ever done to merit such kindness? I think we shall both have to turn over several new leaves and be good.

JOSEPH: Mother and Sister say that the house is in pretty good order, and think that I must have had some extra assistance.

CARRIE: Another basket of pretty things has just been brought in, so I must stop and write another note.

JOSEPH: We shall all be up this evening at the hour specified.

CARRIE: Sarah says when you come, open the sitting room door and go right in (it will be the supper room). Send for her; she wants to speak to you. Come at whatever hour is convenient.... And now, *mon plus cher ami,* my paper is drawing to a close. And I must not keep the bishop of Crete, the emperor of Rome, waiting a moment longer. For the last time, my own beloved—

JOSEPH: For the last time....

CARRIE: For the last time, my dearest, sweetest Joe—goodbye.... What shall I say to you more than I have said? There is but one word that means it all: I love you. I pray for every blessing for my beloved. My prayers are weak, but they are always yours. "The Lord bless thee and keep thee: the Lord make His face shine upon thee and be gracious unto thee: the Lord lift up His countenance upon thee and give thee peace."

FADEOUT

The Night Season

The Night Season is drawn exclusively from the letters of Mary Jones (1808–1869), written from 1854 to 1868, and now preserved in the libraries of the University of Georgia (Athens) and Tulane University (New Orleans).

MRS. MARY JONES, *a lady in middle life*

The scene is set at Montevideo, a rice and cotton plantation in Liberty County, Georgia, some thirty miles southwest of Savannah, from 1854 to 1868.

Act One

After the house lights go down, the voice of Mrs. Mary Jones *is heard in the darkness.*

Montevideo—my happy home! As it now stands it is but the sepulchre of my heart's tenderest loves.... Montevideo.... As I gaze perhaps for the last time upon these woods and groves, these lawns and gardens, these spacious halls where the beloved objects of my life gave happiness to everything around—yes, as I gaze upon them now (all save myself departed) they appear but as the winding sheet of my buried joys.... Montevideo.... Here only on earth do familiar objects unveil the shrouded dead; here only does Memory with her thousand tongues speak to me of the past....

(By now the stage lights have come up, revealing a barely furnished stage. In a moment the voice of Mrs. Mary Jones *is heard offstage, calling.)*

Charles! *(Drawing nearer)* Charles!

*(*Mrs. Mary Jones *enters. She is a handsome, poised, gracious, patrician lady about fifty years old; she is dressed resplendently in the fashion of the 1850's. She looks about for* Charles.*)*

Oh, Charles!

(Seeing her son at last, she comes forward, smiling.)

I do not think, my dear son, that even eighteen months at Cambridge have made you Yankee enough to guess what were the first sounds that saluted our ears this morning: a serenade at sunrise by a traveling minstrel on a hurdy-gurdy.... The whole plantation assembled in delighted wonder to hear "Susannah" and

"Yankee Doodle," and to gaze upon the "great show" of Napoleon laid out in state with his military cap upon his breast. A soldier has raised the pall; an officer stands by gesticulating very solemnly; another keeps guard; whilst at the threshold is a Negro with plate in hand inviting contributions. These figures move with the music, shake their heads and roll their eyes about, and as a piece of money falls into the plate, Congo bobs, turns round, and it disappears in a box behind. This will certainly be a day long to be remembered by the people.

For the last hour I have been roaming about our silent dwelling from room to room, now below stairs, now above, like one whose anxious and sorrowful spirit could not rest. The city of Savannah has suffered beyond description. The Angel of Death has swept every class. Five physicians are reported as dead. Last Sabbath not a church-going bell broke the stillness; the living were all with the dead and dying. In the midst of all this suffering and death the besom of destruction has swept over the city, prostrating houses, uprooting trees, blocking streets. If anything could heighten the scene of woe, it was the horror of darkness which for several nights brooded over the city. The gasworks were so much damaged that their lights were all put out. Only think of the poor sufferers—the sick, the dying, the dead—all shrouded in darkness; not a ray of light with which to administer medicine or catch the farewell look of affection or perform the last sad offices! With what feelings must they have watched for the breaking morn!

Your dear father preached a searching and deeply interesting sermon yesterday in Sunbury: "Follow peace with all men, without which no man shall see the Lord." In the afternoon he gave an exposition of the Ten Commandments to the Negroes.

Sometimes I have hopes that your father is improving; then again I am much discouraged. He has certainly gained flesh, but the nervous inaction continues. Dr. Wells advised blistering the spine for six months. For nearly two I have kept them just below the neck. As soon as they dry up I apply fresh ones each side of the spine and dress with an irritative ointment. This treatment is painful, but your father thinks it beneficial.

We have not yet determined what we shall do in reference to *that family*. We wish to act aright. They have always been unprincipled. Jane gives constant trouble. Much as I should miss the mother, I will not separate them if I can help it. Conscience is better than money. It is a painful and harassing business.

I believe I have never mentioned the marriage of your man William. It was during that dreadful spell of weather. On Sunday morning bright and early, before we had left our chamber, the young couple were announced as below, awaiting the ceremony. We went down and had them brought into the parlor—bride and bridesmaid in swiss muslins with white wreaths on their heads, Sam and William in broadcloth and white gloves. A number of witnesses crowded in. The nuptials being over, I invited the bridal party to retire to the kitchen and partake of a hot breakfast. It was a freezing, shivering morning, and I thought they had displayed a great deal of principle in coming over to be married in the proper manner.

I was glad to see that the infamous proposition to the commercial convention for the revival of the slave trade was promptly rejected. It was a perfect disgrace to the body to present such a subject for consideration.

But it strikes ten o'clock, and I must go. . . . Susan would like to know if you consent to her marrying the man Andrew. I expect it is just as well. I have told her she takes the risk of separation.

(*She addresses her daughter.*)

I think, my dear daughter, you had best buy your winter bonnet at once. And let it be something pretty. How do you like the black-lace or lace-and-velvet bonnets? But I know nothing of the fashions; only please yourself and you will please me. . . . I see Lathrop advertises handsome dress goods; if there is anything you would like to have in the way of a silk or delaine, get it. Whatever you do get, let it be handsome, for you have a plenty of common dresses already. . . . *I* would like one neat morning collar, and two yards of wash blonde for underkerchiefs, and one pair of black kid gloves (you know the size), and some whalebones. And if Lathrop has any of that cheap black velvet (I mean the silk and cotton), I would like enough for a basque.

Do please inquire how much the sewing machines cost, and how they may be obtained. I hear such various accounts of them I am quite puzzled.

Please, my child, say to Sue I was surprised to see your brother's shirts so badly done up. She ironed them with dirty irons. Tell her she must not depend upon Titus, but do the washing herself. And when she breaks off the buttons, she must sew them on again. Even the new shirts are nearly ruined. Tell her I expect to come down and see after things, and your brother's clothes must look very much improved or I shall be very much displeased.

I am distressed, my darling child, to know that your cough still lingers. You must use rubbing and irritants to your chest and between your shoulders night and morning; and get immediately a bottle of Cherry Pectoral and take it faithfully. You know it has done you good on a former occasion, and you must use every means to get rid of that cough at once. Be sure and put on your flannels early.

How much did Mrs. Gilmer's sewing machine cost? A hundred dollars is a great deal to invest in an uncertainty.

Father is shaving and preparing for bed, so I must go. He said just now: "I really believe I have improved some." . . . If it is putting your friends to no inconvenience, my dear, we prefer your coming out with your aunt and uncle. I do not like to see *young ladies* traveling alone in a public stage. . . . You have here a check for twenty dollars; please get it in small sums for housekeeping. And please bring me out four or five loaves of bread; your father enjoys milk toast. . . . Oh—and do not forget my tea. . . . It is verging to midnight. Everything is magnificent without: the full-orbed moon is riding mid-heavens, a cool southeasterly breeze waving the long gray moss and softly sighing amid the boughs of the oaks before the door.

(*She addresses her son.*)

We were very much pleased, my son, to hear of your honorable appointment as judge advocate. It gives me great happiness to hear from various sources of the respect and esteem in which your brother and yourself are held, professionally and socially. Character is everything to a young man.... This morning I read the 7th Chapter of Proverbs: "Wherewithal shall a young man cleanse his way? By taking heed thereto according to Thy Word." It grieves my heart to know that you are not a Christian; but it would break it—it would break it—to hear of you or your brother what is said of most young men in cities.

It has rained the whole day, and the chapel service has been a sad one: the funeral of our poor servant-woman Sina. On Sabbath as we returned from church we found her in bed with fever. The usual remedies not succeeding, we called in young Dr. Way, who did not consider her case dangerous. Yesterday morning she lost an infant. The doctor was with us all day, and when he left just before sunset he did not express any special fears about her situation. Your father rode over at nine o'clock and said he saw no change except a profuse perspiration. He returned to the house but a short time when he was summoned back; and she died at ten o'clock without a struggle.... Eve left four children, and Sina leaves five. Nine motherless ones now to be cared for! You know the tenderness of your father's feelings, and his ceaseless anxiety when the servants are sick. They tell most sensibly, and he is more unwell than for a great while: the nervous inaction greatly increased.

Your father and myself think with you, my dear son, that if $4300 can be realized for *that family,* you had best close the bargain at once. Of course, as we are compelled to sell, we would like to realize their value, but are willing to let them go for less in view of selling all together. We are now much in want of funds to meet our liabilities in bank. I know that you will do the best for us in this matter. It will be a relief to have the business closed; it has caused me great distress.

You have an addition to your servants. Clarissa has a very large daughter. I have supplied all her wants but a blanket. We have for many years made it a practice to give a blanket to every newborn infant as a kind of bonus to the mother. If you say so, I will give her one of the blankets sent out from Savannah.

Old Daddy Tony returns you "tousand tanks" for the tobacco. It was a cold damp evening when I took it around to the old man. He had not left his house in consequence of the cold for several days, and was sitting over the fire when I entered and told him I had brought him a present from his young master. When I handed it over, he rose from his seat, his eye kindling, and exclaimed: "God bless my young master! He never forgets the old man! Do, Missis, give him tousand tanks." They pride themselves upon the fact that the tobacco is put up in a paper. I have never the least toleration for the weed except in cases of happiness conferred upon some old mama or daddy.

The death of Mrs. Sorrel was very distressing. We are not sufficiently grateful for our preserved reason. Our commonest blessings are our greatest; we need only to be deprived of them to feel it is so. But few remain of those whom we consider aged. I begin to realize that your father and myself will soon be in the front ranks, pressing onward to the grave! Last Saturday was my birthday, and I have numbered my half century.

It is now very late; I have received several calls and messages and must go.... I feel very anxious on your dear father's account. His appetite is very poor, with a tendency to the old throat affection. My only solace is in looking unto the Great Physician; with Him alone are the issues of life and death.

(*She addresses her daughter.*)

I have risen a half hour earlier than usual. The sun in all his glory is just above the trees, and his brilliant rays, darting through the deep green foliage of the old cedar in the yard, fall with fanciful effect all around me.... I dreamed of you, my dear child, last night. I hope Robert is taking good care of you. We were very happy to know that you are a useful wife. You must not allow your domestic duties to absorb all your time, but give a due share to mental culture. And do not neglect your music; we long to hear you play and sing. How degrading to the intellect is the way in which young females particularly spend their time! With the mass of mankind there seems very little conscientious improvement of the talents—for which they will have to render an account.

It gratifies us to know that you receive such kind attentions from your friends and neighbors; and I hope, my dear child, that you will not be wanting in any conduct or feeling that will entitle you to respect and affection as a minister's wife. Be kind to all. Neglect none, especially those who rank amongst the poor and humble. I do not think it any disadvantage that you have gone almost a stranger into your husband's congregation. Indulge no prejudices. Form no intimacies. If you seek to do good, the way will ever be opened to you. All else but the time we have spent in doing good will vanish as a dream when we take our last review of life's pilgrimage.

I cannot begin to tell you how much we miss you. I try to console myself with the reflection that the happiness of my children should be my happiness, but this philosophy does not always still the heart's yearning. I dread the alienation which long separations produce even with the nearest and dearest.

Breakfast waits.... I hope you have a comfortable house for your servant Lucy. You must not forget her welfare, for she is an excellent woman, and I think will be faithful to you.... I am really grieved Kate has acted so. Tell her I hope if possible she will marry the man and try and lead a better life.

(*She addresses her son.*)

My dear son, the incident you so beautifully describe of the Negroes' singing at Dr. Wayne's funeral was one of the most touching I ever heard of. If it be dreadful to have the cry of the poor and the oppressed rising up to God against us, how sweet like incense poured forth their tributes of gratitude and affection!... One of the precious recollections of my own dear mother was her unvarying kindness to the poor and needy, which to their dying day embalmed her memory in their hearts.

Scarcely have I had a moment in the last three weeks. I have been the sole nurse of your dear sister and the little baby. We wish you could see your sweet little niece just as she is. We have thought at times she resembled you in your infancy. She is not large, but well formed, and fat as a ricebird, is strong and healthy, has never had a colic, and has the best appetite you can imagine. And your dear sister has such an abundance of nourishment she has had to nurse one of the little Negroes. I observed the nine-days rule in bed strictly, and as you suggested, kept her very quiet for over two weeks. She now takes a short ride every morning, and dined with us for the first time today.

Be assured, my dear child, of your parents' warmest sympathy at this time. It is a new era in our country's history, and I trust the wise and patriotic leaders of the people will soon devise some united course of action throughout the Southern states. I cannot see a shadow of reason for civil war in the event of a Southern confederacy; but even that, if it must come, would be preferable to submission to Black Republicanism, involving as it would all that is horrible and degrading and ruinous. "Forbearance has ceased to be a virtue"; and I believe we could meet with no evils out of the Union that would compare to those we will finally suffer if we continue in it; for we can no longer doubt that the settled policy of the North is to crush the South.

An indescribable sadness weighs down my soul as I think of our once glorious but now dissolving Union. Our children's children—what will constitute *their* national pride and glory? We have no alternative; and necessity demands that we now protect ourselves from entire destruction at the hands of those who have torn and rent and obliterated every national bond of union and confidence and affection.... When your brother and yourself were very little fellows, we took you into old Independence Hall; and at the foot of Washington's statue I pledged you both to support and defend the Union. That Union has passed away, and you are free from your mother's vow.

Did your father tell you old Montevideo gave forth her response on the night of the 26th in sympathy with Savannah? Strange to say, as we walked out to view the illumination from the lawn, we discovered there were thirteen windows on the front of the house, each of which had one brilliant light resembling a star; and without design one of them had been placed far in the ascendant—emblematic, as we hailed it, of the noble and gallant state which must ever be regarded as the polar star of our Southern confederacy.

We shall no doubt soon be surrounded by all the horrors of war. In my poor way I want to testify my interest in those who are called to defend our homes and firesides, our lives and liberties. I have had all the sage and balm from the garden dried, and if you think it would be acceptable I will send it for the sick. And following out the suggestions of the governor, I would like to prepare clothing for four soldiers.

Our hearts are filled with gratitude to God for our victory over our enemies, and at the same time we weep at the costly sacrifice. I have never realized before that the malicious fanaticism of the North could extend to such organized and practical results. It is no longer a war of words.... Here is twenty dollars. Please forward it as you know best to some official in Richmond for the use of our suffering and wounded soldiers. I wish it was an hundredfold. There is nothing in this world too good for those who are shedding their precious blood and giving their lives to protect us from ruin and misery.

Many thanks, my dear son, for the delightful tea. It is the only article of luxury I ever crave. We will have to touch such luxuries daintily if the blockade lasts. One thing is certain: we will endure privations joyfully rather than yield an inch to the vile miscreants now seeking our destruction.

Savannah is still said to be in a defenseless condition! Not a gun on the water approaches! Of course I know nothing of the matter—saving that the mistakes of our commanding general have now to be rectified in hot haste at the last moment, and that his name is never mentioned with either respect or confidence as a military leader. *Why* in such a state of public sentiment and public peril is he not at once superseded, and someone of judgment, ability, and tried valor placed in his stead?

This is your third night in camp, and my thoughts have dwelt with you, within those thin cloth coverings wet with the dews and rains. Your couch perhaps has been the damp earth, and sad fears for your health amid such exposures are rising up before me. Oh, this cruel, cruel war! I am every moment forced to feel it has been so from the commencement, in sympathy with my suffering relatives and countrymen; but now it is brought to my own bosom when yielding up my beloved sons.

I feel that you have both acted noble parts in going into active service upon the tented field. You, my son, might have yielded to the solicitations of your fellow citizens in continuing in the discharge of high and honorable duties, surrounded by the comforts of home. But it has been your choice to lay these aside and share every hardship and privation with your gallant company.

I know that you are now every moment exposed to the attack of our perfidious and merciless enemy; but your sword will be drawn in a righteous cause, and I fervently implore my God to protect and save you in the day of battle, and to strengthen your arms for the conflict, that in your full measure you may be enabled to repel the invaders who are now at our own doors with their work of ruin and destruction. Their intentions are now openly declared, and nothing but Omnipotent Power will keep them from making this not only a civil but a servile war.

(*She addresses her daughter.*)

Yesterday, my dear daughter, we heard of the death of Willie Howe at Centreville. He was in the battle of July 21st. A noble, gallant youth. Such are the priceless treasures this vile enemy demands and receives from our hearts and homes.

The hour has arrived when men and women too in the Southern confederacy must seek to do their duty with fearless hearts and hands. Our recent disasters are appalling. The thought of Nashville, the heart of the country and I may say granary of our Confederacy, falling into the hands of those robbers and murderers casts a terrible gloom over us all. I trust this day's mail will bring us some encouraging news!

Eight of Joe Anderson's Negroes left him on Sunday night. Their leader was his man James, who was cooking for the picket guard in Sunbury; and while they either slept or ceased to watch on Sunday night he took the picket boat and packed it with his own family and friends and left them minus breakfast on Monday morning! To mend the matter James's daughter went into the house and packed up all of Eva's best clothes and jewelry in her own trunk and took them away with her!

I trust ere this the little darling has been relieved. I used always to give you when children a simple remedy for colds and hoarseness: linseed oil and honey. We used to keep it mixed, and if you woke in the night with a croupy cough you were sure to be dosed. I have never used anything else with white or black. Linseed oil and honey. A teaspoonful at a time is enough for an infant.

My darling, do not let her kiss the little dog: it is dangerous. You know dogs may have symptoms of hydrophobia before we know it.

(*She addresses her son.*)

I am all alone this evening. Everything around me exhibits a scene of perfect tranquillity. The trees with their deep dark shadows are reposing upon the lawn, which is irradiated with the soft pure light of a half-grown moon; whilst the melodious notes of the whippoorwill, unfailing harbinger of spring returned and winter gone, are echoing from the grove near the house and reechoing from the distant wood. In strange contrast to all that is beautiful and peaceful in this dear home of ours is the "rude sound of war's alarms" as it breaks even now upon my ear from the cannon's slow and measured thunderstrokes. Oh, the agony that comes over me at times! Where is my child? I trust Fort Pulaski will stand out against an attack.

Your dear father has contracted a violent cold, and is now scarcely able to speak. You have no conception, my son, how feeble he is. At times he appears very despondent in reference to his future recovery. His life and health are beyond every other consideration to me.

The fall of Fort Pulaski after so short a bombardment, and the surrender of the garrison without even an attempt at escape and blowing up of the fort, which certainly could have been done, appears both astounding and humiliating! The state of our long-neglected defenses and the results, now to be fatally realized, of ignorance, imbecility, and neglect make us see when too late for remedy the ruin and misery brought upon us by the general in command, who has had since this time last year to occupy and fortify the positions taken by our enemies within the past four or five months and now used for our destruction. How dark the clouds are hanging all over our beloved country! The Righteous Judge alone knows the end from the beginning!

Night, dark and rainy, closes in. Your dear father has been very much weakened by his recent cold. Today I have packed several trunks with necessary clothing, and shall try and prepare for emergencies; for emphatically we know not what a day may bring forth.

We received the extra, and I have not words to express the emotions I feel at this signal success in the last fearful assault of our enemies, who have arrayed a force five or six to one, armed with all the deadly appliances of modern warfare, to overwhelm and destroy us. I feel thankful that in this great struggle the head of our army is a noble son of Virginia, and worthy of the intimate relation in which he stands connected with our immortal Washington. What confidence his wisdom and integrity and valor and undoubted piety inspire! And Virginia—noble Virginia—although she delayed her action in the offset, has bravely bared her bosom to the storm. Oh, that our God would speedily establish us as a nation in righteousness and peace!

Your father has passed a very bad night, and I consider him critically ill. I know not if your brother could possibly come, but wish you to telegraph him as early as you can. Your father has objected to sending for the physicians in the county; and I am well aware if his true situation was not understood by them, rash practice would be injurious if not fatal.... I cannot express the anxieties that are weighing upon my heart.... Telegraph Joe immediately: he is evidently growing more and more feeble. May God strengthen and uphold us all!

FADEOUT

Act Two

As the stage lights come up, MRS. MARY JONES, *wearing black, is seated at a desk, writing. She addresses her daughter.*

I am in the study today, with aching head, and far more aching heart, trying to gather up the cherished recollections of your honored father, my tenderly beloved husband; my blinding tears now and then forcing me to stop and ask: "Of whom am I writing? Can it be true that I shall nevermore behold his face on earth?"

I am as one struggling to awake from a terrible dream. I know that our loss is his eternal gain; but oh, when no returning footstep falls upon my listening ear, no voice of love and kindness, no cheerful greeting, no words of counsel and encouragement—that empty chair, that vacant sofa where first we plighted our early vows, that desk where he labored so perseveringly, his Bible left open upon it, his spectacles just as he laid them down, his hat, his stick just as he placed them on the table in the entry—can you wonder that I longed to be here with all these precious memorials around me?

I could but admire the ingenuity of my servants today in the case of a suspicious-looking character who came up and asked for food. They told him their master lived in Savannah, and they could not entertain him. They asked that I would not come down. I told them I could not send him hungry away, and ordered Kate to get some dinner for him. They made him sit in the piazza, and when he attempted to come into the house (as he said, "to see how it looked") Flora and Tom barred the front door. I could see him from the balcony, and when his dinner was ready they sent him by

Charles a large plate of rice and pork, with a bowl of clabber, and would not even trust him with a knife and fork, but gave him only an iron spoon. The poor fellow eat* voraciously—the first, he said, in three days. When he finished, Charles politely told him if he would start now he would put him on the right road. I hope I did not violate any law of charity or humanity, but I had not the courage to let him remain. Charles and Tom managed so well I gave them each a little reward.

The death of our pious, brave, and noble General Stonewall Jackson is a great blow to our cause! May God raise up friends and helpers to our bleeding country! How *long* will this awful conflict last? And to what depths of misery are we to be reduced ere the Sovereign Judge of all the earth will give us deliverance? I do bless God for the spirit of true patriotism and undaunted courage with which He is arming us for this struggle. Noble Vicksburg! From her heroic example we gather strength to hold on and hold out to the last moment. I can look extinction for me and mine in the face, but *submission* never! It would be degradation of the lowest order.

(*She addresses her son.*)

Today, my dear son, I shall send for you, through the distributing commissary of Savannah, a basket of provisions containing a boiled ham, biscuits, butter, potatoes, green sweet oranges, one dozen candles, and a bottle of blackberry prepared for medicinal use (excellent for all bowel affections—prepared with brandy, consequently a strong article). In the basket I have put a few Testaments and tracts.... Let me tell you here, my son, that I am prepared to come to you at a moment's warning; and should you suffer in any way by wounds or disease, nothing shall keep me away from you. And I hope you will never deceive me about yourself.

These are dark days! Our army seems in peril at so many points. I can but regard as the darkest sign of the times this talk of reconstruction and submission, and the spirit of speculation,

---

*Pronounced *ĕt*: archaic form of *ate*.

fattening upon the miseries and wants of a suffering land. I bless the Lord every day of my life that I am not a houseless wanderer as thousands of my noble countrywomen are, but am still surrounded with the comforts of life. And what is far above all these things, the lives of my beloved children are still spared whilst so many are mourning their loved ones slain upon the battlefield or laid in their graves by the hand of disease.

Last night I felt the loneliness of my situation to an unusual degree. Not a white female of my acquaintance nearer than the depot! Oh, my son, the desolation of heart which I feel is beyond expression! The death of your beloved father every day presses more and more heavily upon me. Yesterday was the anniversary of his fifty-ninth birthday, today the thirty-third of our marriage. And it was just such a cold, cloudless, brilliant December day as this. It was the first breath of winter upon the beautiful autumn flowers that had lingered in the garden and were gathered to deck the bridal hall. That scene is the reality in which I live. Today I walked alone upon that beautiful lawn. I sat upon the blocks where he used to mount his horse. I stood beneath the trees his own hands had trimmed. I listened to the song of the sweet birds he loved so well. I could not pass the day without a visit to our precious dead. All was sunlight: no shadows resting on their graves. This afternoon I read: "Eye hath not seen, nor ear heard, neither have entered into the heart of man the things which God hath prepared for them that love Him." Our beloved ones now see and hear and know.

Not a line from you for more than a week! What suspense hangs upon every hour! And what a relief when the mailbag reveals a letter in your own handwriting!

You have never told me who compose your mess. General Taliaferro is a Virginian, of course. In 1847, when we visited Virginia, one very charming day we took a trip down the James River, and on board the steamer made the acquaintance of a young U.S. officer of that name. I think he was then on a recruiting service for the Mexican War. We always cherished a very pleasant recollection of the kind attentions which he showed us in pointing out the many magnificent estates that then graced the hillsides bordering the river. To this day the green heights of Shirley and the cultivated fields of Brandon are before my mind's eye. Alas, for the change which has passed over them! I have a kind of fancy that your general may once have been that young officer.

Last night I had a dream that caused me great anguish in sleep, and I woke up shivering as though I had a chill. I thought your dear father had died, and they were taking him away without permitting me to look upon his face!

For several days we have had weeping skies, and now the rain is falling fast. It *comforts* me to feel that the winds and the waves may be made instruments for our defense by Him who holds them in His almighty hand. Then again I think of my poor boy beneath the thin cloth tent, or exposed upon the open field to the tempest if not to the deadly fire of the inhuman foe.

Today I feel unusually depressed about our future prospects: the occupation of Chattanooga by General Rosecrans and his fortifying and making it the base of operations; the giving up of one important point after another by General Bragg, falling back all the time with the delusive expectation of some advantage to be gained. It may all be right; I am of course incapable of judging. But thus it appears. And if we have not the power to prevent the enemy from occupying our strongholds, how are we ever to dislodge them and drive them out when once they have gained possession? Their advances upon our territory are fearful!

Do not, my dear son, suppose that my spirit quails beneath the dark clouds which appear to curtain our political horizon on almost every side. No. I believe we are contending for a just and righteous cause; and I would infinitely prefer that we *all* perish in its defense before we submit to the infamy and disgrace and utter ruin and misery involved in any connection whatever with the vilest and most degraded nation on the face of the earth.

Present my respects to the general. I am happy to know that you are associated with a gentleman of whom we formed so pleasant an impression; and the position he now occupies proves his country's estimate of his worth and ability. I do not wonder that he remembered your beloved father, for I think no one could forget his appearance and manners. Oh, my child, this afternoon the *truth* that he is not here—that I shall no more behold him in mortal flesh—came over me with awful power as I went to the vacant study!

Every prospect darkens round us. The fearful condition of our armies on the front of our own state and Virginia fills every heart with trembling. Not a day now passes but we receive the sad tidings of some friend or acquaintance slain in battle. Colonel Joe McAllister is said to have died bravely. He was surrounded by the enemy, who demanded his surrender. He replied: "Only with life!" and continued to shoot down the enemy until overpowered. His last act was to hurl his pistol at their heads.

(*She addresses her daughter.*)

Will you be kind enough, my child, to send my candle molds. My lights have almost gone out, and I must try and prepare for nights of darkness.

I am perplexed about this house. Ought the furniture to be removed? All that I have is here. If the enemy advance upon the railroad, I will be constantly exposed here to stragglers. I try to be calm and hopeful, but sometimes my heart almost dies within me. Those who have food and shelter and quiet homes in a protected region have reason for special gratitude.

A keen northwester is sweeping over the lawn and whistling among the trees, from the branches of which the long gray moss is waving. The pall of death is suddenly cast over our once cheerful and happy home. Not a living creature stirs in garden or yard, on the plain or in the grove. Nature wears a funereal aspect, and the blast, as it sweeps through the branches, is sighing a requiem to departed days.

As I stand and look at the desolating changes wrought by the hand of an inhuman foe in a few days, I can enter into the feelings of Job when he exclaimed: "Naked came I out of my mother's womb, and naked shall I return thither; the Lord gave, and the Lord hath taken away: blessed be the name of the Lord." All our pleasant things are laid low. Lover and friend is put far from us, and our acquaintance into darkness. We are prisoners in our own home; we dare not open windows or doors. Sometimes our little children are allowed under a strict watch and guard to run in the sunshine, but it is always under constant apprehension. The poor little creatures at a moment's warning—just let them hear "Yankee coming!"—rush in and remain almost breathless, huddled together in one of the upper rooms like a bevy of frightened partridges. To obtain a mouthful of food we have been obliged to cook in what was formerly our drawing room; and I have to rise every morning by candlelight, before the dawn of day, that we may have it before the enemy arrives to take it from us. And then sometimes we and the dear little ones have not a chance to eat again before dark. The poor servants are harassed to death, going rapidly for wood or water and hurrying in to lock the doors, fearing insults and abuse at every turn. Do the annals of civilized—and I may add savage—warfare afford any record of brutality equaled in extent and duration to that which has been inflicted on us by the Yankees?

One thing is evident: they are now enlisting the Negroes here in their service. As one of the officers said to me, "We do not want your women, but we mean to take the able-bodied men to dredge out the river and harbor at Savannah, to hew timber, make roads, build bridges, and throw up batteries." They offer twelve dollars per month. Many are going off with them. Some few sensible ones calculate the value of twelve dollars per month in furnishing food and clothing and fuel and lodging. Up to this time none from this place has joined them. I have told some of those indisposed to help in any way and to wander off at pleasure that as they were perfectly useless here it would be best for me and for the good of their fellow servants if they would go at once with the Yankees. They had seen what their conduct was to the black people—stealing from them, searching their houses, cursing and abusing and insulting their wives and daughters; and if they chose such for their masters to obey and follow, then the sooner they went with them the better; and I had quite a mind to send in a request that they be carried off.

The workings of Providence in reference to the African race are truly wonderful. The scourge falls with peculiar weight upon them: with their emancipation must come their extermination. All history, from their first existence, proves them incapable of self-government; they perish when brought in conflict with the intellectual superiority of the Caucasian race. Northern philanthropy may rave as much as it pleases; but facts prove that in a state of slavery such as exists in the South has the Negro race increased and thriven most. Not that we have done our duty to them here; far from it. I feel if ever we gain our independence there will be radical reforms in the system of slavery as it now exists. When once delivered from the interference of Northern abolitionism, we shall be free to make and enforce such rules and reformations as are just and right. In all my life I never heard such expressions of hatred and contempt as the Yankees heap upon our poor servants. One of them told me he did not know what God Almighty made Negroes for; all he wished was the power to blow their brains out.

In our captivity we are in utter ignorance of all without. We know not the state of our cause or the condition of affairs in the Confederacy. Clouds and darkness are round about us; the hand of the Almighty is laid in sore judgment upon us; we are a desolated and smitten people. The enemy are in full possession of Savannah; Negroes in large numbers are flocking to them. We fear our poor army is in a bad way. General Hood is reported almost annihilated, and supplies for General Lee's army greatly diminished. What is to be our social and civil status we cannot see.

(*She addresses her son.*)

Your last letter, my dear son, was not received until yesterday. It had evidently been *torn* open. This, I am told, is now frequently done to ascertain the sentiments of the people; so we will have to use great prudence.

We are passing through fearful times. Large numbers of Negroes have returned to the county—some six hundred, it is said, already; and instigated by Cato, the people at Montevideo have behaved in such a way that Mr. Fennell has been forced to call in the Yankees. Cato has been to me a most insolent, indolent, and dishonest man; I have not a shadow of confidence in him, and will not wish to retain him on the place. Dear as my sweet home has been, if suitable arrangements cannot be made for my remaining here and having it under cultivation, I may be compelled to part with it.

Robert has taken the oath; and as I have several interests to represent, would it not be well for me to do so at once?

(*She takes the oath.*)

"I do solemnly affirm, in the presence of Almighty God, that I will henceforth faithfully support, protect, and defend the Constitution of the United States and the union of the states thereunder, and that I will in like manner abide by and faithfully support all laws and proclamations which have been made during the existing rebellion with reference to the emancipation of slaves. So help me God."

(*She addresses her daughter.*)

I cannot sleep—I cannot sleep. I have been lying awake thinking of you all, and now rise and light the lamp. Your letters, my darling child, are a great comfort to me in this far-off wilderness. We still have no mails, and it is only as some kind friend brings me a letter that I hear from my children.

The past has been a week of trial. Sam (Sue's husband) came from Savannah and announced his intention of taking her to a farm near Savannah. I spoke with Sue and reminded her of Sam's want of fidelity to her, and the unjust and unkind manner in which he had often treated her. She, however, decided to go; and I told her if so, I preferred she should go at once; whereupon she withdrew Elizabeth in the midst of our last rice-cutting, and they have been for a week walking about at large. I told Sue if she was ever in want or ill-treated, she must return to me. She replied: "No, ma'am, I'll never come back, for you told me to go," thus in a saucy way perverting my remark. Although Sue has been disrespectful to me and shown a very perverse spirit, I do remember all her former fidelity; and I am truly sorry for her, for I believe she will feel the loss of her comfortable home. Flora announced if her aunty went she would not stay by herself, so I presume when it suits her convenience she too will go. Even Gilbert (through his wife Fanny) has the matter of change under consideration. But I am thoroughly disgusted with the whole race. I could fill my sheet with details of dishonesty at Montevideo, but my heart sickens at the recital.

My precious child, I think of you constantly and wish you had one-half of this large and comfortable home and furniture. When you will ever be able to get anything from here is uncertain, as they are so slow in completing the Central Railroad. I have no doubt many things could be sold—if people could pay for them. It is very painful to me to know that I have it not in my power to aid my dear children, and that they have all to struggle hard to maintain their families. It is with peculiar sorrow that I think, my dear child, of your uncomfortable situation—not even a carpet on your floor or a pair of andirons in your chimney, and the severe winter soon to set in.

As I told you, Sue had left. Flora is in a most unhappy condition, doing very little, and that poorly. I overheard an amusing conversation between Cook Kate and herself: they are looking forward to gold watches and chains, bracelets, and blue veils and silk dresses! Jack has entered a boardinghouse in Savannah, where I presume he will act the Congo gentleman to perfection. I shall cease my anxieties for the race. My life long (I mean since I had a home) I have been caring for them; and since the war I have labored with all my might to supply their wants, and expended everything I had upon their support, directly or indirectly; and this is their return.

You can have no idea of their deplorable state. They are perfectly deluded: will not enter into any engagement for another year, and will not work *now* except as it pleases them. Several of them refuse positively to do *any* work. My heart is pained with their vileness and falsehood in every way. I long to be delivered from the race. At times my heart is so heavy I feel I cannot remain. But I have no other home, and if I desert it, everything will go to ruin.

Last night there was a large meeting and registering of names at Riceboro. A Yankee Negro the speaker. Assurances given that the coming year forty acres of land would be given to each, and *our* lands confiscated and given to them, to whom they justly belonged. A fearful state of things! Where will it end?

I sometimes feel I must sink under the various perplexities of this situation. I have struggled hard to bear up under the severe losses, the sad reverses, and I may almost say pecuniary ruin of our temporal prospects. But I feel that God is hedging up my way here; and I have come to the determination that if a purchaser can be found, we must part with our beloved, our long-cherished home. I do not see how I can keep it up, dependent as I am upon a manager for the oversight and upon the false and faithless freedmen as laborers. If there was hope of improvement in the future, I could endure any temporary trials; but I am convinced that the condition of things will grow worse and worse. There is nothing to make it better—at least with the present generation; and by what means the Negro is to be elevated to an intelligent and reliable laborer I cannot see. The whole constitution of the race is adverse to responsibility, to truth, to industry. He can neglect duty and violate contracts without the least compunction of conscience or loss of honor; and he can sink to the lowest depths of want and misery without any sense of shame.

Last Sabbath was a deeply solemn and sorrowful day at Midway Church. Our beloved and faithful pastor, connected with us for thirteen years and four months, broke to us the emblems of our Redeemer's love for the last time. Tuesday at one o'clock the cars came; and it was an affecting sight to see him leaving, and a long line of weeping and sorrowing ladies and gentlemen and young men and children left at the side of the vacant track, now sheep without a shepherd. For the first time in the history of our venerated sanctuary the living teacher is withdrawn. So far as we are concerned, silence will reign within those consecrated walls. And our precious dead must sleep in the solitude and neglect of a wilderness.

It is true, my child, this county is in ruins. The people are becoming poorer and poorer; I know not what is to become of them. My situation here is just this: one bale of cotton and about twenty bushels of corn made by the freedmen employed. And a salary of four hundred dollars to pay the manager! I had a talk with him last night and offered to turn everything into his hands, but he will not hear to it; and although I have furnished everything besides for his support and comfort in health and sickness, and he has really done nothing so far as labor is concerned on the place, he has not the honor or conscience to say he is willing to share in any degree the total loss of the year.

And now you must write me the best way of going to New Orleans, and what it will cost to take me there. If I only had the means, I would send you just what you need to furnish your house. Would you be willing to pay the express on the Philadelphia sofa and the six chairs to match? I *must* bring on your father's papers; I could not leave them. All else—books, pictures, bedding—must remain. Do write at once—and particularly; I have not a moment to spare.

I have risen at midnight and thrown wide the closed shutters of my chamber window, that I might look once more upon my beautiful earthly home. The clear bright moon is approaching its full-orbed proportions. From the diadem of night is reflected the magnificent light of countless brilliant stars. Jupiter sits unrivaled upon his imperial throne. Orion displays his martial belt of peerless gems. Beautiful Venus still veils her matchless charms behind the orient sky, waiting to harbinger the coming moon.

Nature below is in perfect repose. Not the faintest zephyr stirs the sleeping forest leaves. The giant oaks and lofty pines are perfectly daguerreotyped upon the lawn, whilst the pure white walks of the garden stand out like silvery highways. Not a sound is heard to break the profound stillness of midnight, saving an occasional tinkle of the bell as Pretty Maid shakes her head or changes her place in the cow pen, or our faithful gander, who keeps his sentry watch in the poultry yard, calls out the passing hour.

What a skeleton world has this now become to me! The bright prisms of hope which once encircled every object and gilded every scene have faded tint by tint. Of earthly possessions and enjoyments I have seen an end; riches have taken to themselves wings and flown away; I am a captive in the home I love, and soon must wander from it—an exile in my native land.

When first we came to this now beautiful home, it was a rough and uncultivated field. The spacious dwelling has been built and every improvement has been made under our own eye; every tree and flower has been planted by our own hand. That beautiful cedar in front of the dwelling was planted by my husband; I see him bending to the task. That magnificent live oak, from which a twig was never cut, was set out by our faithful house servant Jack before his own cottage door. Old Daddy Jupiter planted that leaning oak at the turn of the avenue "to be remembered by."

These living memorials remain, but the hands that placed them there are moldering where "no work nor device is found." The halls of this mansion no longer echo to the master's step. The chair is vacant at the board and around the hearthstone. The precious study is closed, the desk unused and the books all packed. The servants that used so faithfully and pleasantly to wait around us are dead or scattered or sadly changed. "The adversary hath spread out his hand upon all our pleasant things." His robberies and oppressions force me from my beloved home, where it is no longer safe or prudent to remain. And I must leave it in my advancing years, knowing not where the gray hairs which sorrow and time have thickly gathered will find a shelter, or any spot that I may ever again on earth call home.

"My God, my God, why hast thou forsaken me? Why art thou so far from helping me? . . . O my God, I cry in the daytime, but thou hearest me not; and in the night season, and am not silent.... Our fathers trusted in thee: they trusted, and thou didst deliver them.... Be not thou far from me, O Lord: O my strength, haste thee to help me."

Thus far, my darling child, am I spared on my way to you. The closing up of my life at home has been very painful. You will know when I ought to arrive, and I know Robert will meet me at the depot. Oh, how I dread the undertaking! It seems so strange! If I only knew someone to call upon in Mobile to see me on the steamer!... I have engaged a marble slab, and leave an inscription to be placed upon it. Wish I could have consulted you all, but I could not leave your father's grave uncared for, and I have done the best I could.

FADEOUT

A Note on the Author

Robert Manson Myers received the National Book Award for *The Children of Pride* in 1973. He is Professor of English Emeritus at the University of Maryland.